Shell Shocked: Learn Bash for Cybersecurity and Automation

Rick Stupart

Published by ELC Publishing, 2026.

SHELL SHOCKED: LEARN BASH FOR CYBERSECURITY AND AUTOMATION

First edition. September 2, 2026.

ISBN: 979-8235962446

Written by Rick Stupart.

Table of Contents

Introduction: Why Bash Matters in Cybersecurity

In the rapidly evolving landscape of cybersecurity, where threats emerge at lightning speed and defensive measures must adapt just as quickly, one tool has remained consistently powerful and indispensable: the Bash shell. While flashy graphical interfaces and sophisticated security platforms capture headlines, the humble command line continues to serve as the backbone of cybersecurity operations worldwide. For security professionals, penetration testers, system administrators, and automation engineers, Bash scripting represents far more than just a convenient way to execute commands—it's the foundation upon which efficient, scalable, and reliable security operations are built.

The importance of Bash in cybersecurity cannot be overstated. In an industry where time is often the difference between preventing a breach and containing a disaster, the ability to automate repetitive tasks, rapidly analyze system configurations, and deploy countermeasures across multiple systems simultaneously can mean the difference between success and failure. Bash provides this capability through its unique position as both a command interpreter and a powerful scripting language, offering direct access to the underlying operating system while maintaining the flexibility to create complex automation workflows.

This introduction will establish why Bash scripting has become an essential skill for cybersecurity professionals and how mastering it can transform your approach to security tasks. We'll explore the fundamental advantages that make Bash indispensable in security operations, examine the real-world scenarios where Bash scripting provides significant advantages over other tools, and guide you through setting up a proper learning environment where you can safely practice and experiment with the techniques you'll learn throughout this book.

The Power of the Shell: Bash as Your First Hacking and Automation Tool

The Bash shell represents one of the most powerful and versatile tools available to cybersecurity professionals, serving as both a gateway to system administration and a sophisticated automation platform. Understanding why Bash holds this unique position requires examining both its technical capabilities and its practical applications in security contexts. Unlike graphical user interfaces that limit you to predefined options and workflows, Bash provides direct, unfettered access to the operating system's core functionality, allowing you to interact with files, processes, network connections, and system resources in ways that GUI tools simply cannot match.

The Foundation of System Control

At its core, Bash serves as the primary interface between human operators and Unix-like operating systems, including Linux distributions that form the backbone of most enterprise security infrastructures. This fundamental role gives Bash users unprecedented control over system behavior, from managing file permissions and process execution to configuring network settings and monitoring system performance. For cybersecurity professionals, this level of control translates directly into the ability to implement security measures, investigate potential threats, and respond to incidents with precision and speed that graphical tools cannot provide.

The shell's text-based nature, while initially intimidating to newcomers, represents one of its greatest strengths in security applications. Text-based interfaces are inherently more scriptable, more reliable across different system configurations, and more efficient in terms of both system resources and network bandwidth. When you're investigating a security incident on a remote server over a slow connection, or when you need to execute the same security check across hundreds of systems, the efficiency and consistency of command-line operations become invaluable advantages.

Automation Capabilities and Scripting Power

Bash's scripting capabilities transform it from a simple command interpreter into a full-featured programming environment specifically designed for system administration and automation tasks. The language includes all the fundamental programming constructs you'd expect—variables, loops, conditional statements, functions, and error handling—while maintaining seamless integration with the vast ecosystem of Unix command-line tools. This integration means that any command you can execute interactively at the shell prompt can be incorporated into a script, creating powerful automation workflows that combine multiple tools and techniques.

The automation potential of Bash scripting in cybersecurity contexts is virtually limitless. You can create scripts that automatically scan network ranges for specific vulnerabilities, monitor log files for suspicious patterns, backup critical system configurations before making security changes, or deploy security updates across multiple systems simultaneously. These automation capabilities don't just save time—they also improve consistency and reduce the likelihood of human error in critical security operations.

Integration with Security Tools and Ecosystems

One of Bash's most significant advantages in cybersecurity work is its seamless integration with the broader ecosystem of security tools and utilities. Most command-line security tools, from network scanners like Nmap to vulnerability assessment frameworks like OpenVAS, are designed to work efficiently with shell scripts. This integration allows you to create comprehensive security workflows that combine multiple tools, process their outputs, and make decisions based on the results—all within a single script.

The pipe and redirection operators built into Bash enable sophisticated data processing workflows where the output of one security tool becomes the input for another, creating analysis pipelines that would be difficult or impossible to replicate in graphical environments. For example, you might use Bash to orchestrate a workflow where Nmap discovers active hosts on a network, feeds those results to a vulnerability scanner, processes the scanner output to identify critical issues, and then automatically generates formatted reports for different stakeholders.

Resource Efficiency and Scalability

In cybersecurity operations, resource efficiency often directly correlates with operational effectiveness. Bash scripts typically consume minimal system resources compared to graphical applications or interpreted languages with heavy runtime environments. This efficiency becomes critical when you're running security tools on resource-constrained systems, processing large datasets, or executing operations across many systems simultaneously.

The scalability advantages of Bash become apparent when dealing with enterprise-scale security operations. A well-written Bash script can process thousands of log entries, scan hundreds of network hosts, or configure security settings across dozens of systems using the same computational resources that might be required for a single equivalent operation in a less efficient environment. This scalability makes Bash an ideal choice for implementing security measures that need to operate effectively at enterprise scale.

Learning Curve and Skill Development

Despite its power and flexibility, Bash maintains a relatively gentle learning curve that makes it accessible to cybersecurity professionals at all skill levels. The language's syntax is straightforward and readable, with clear relationships between commands and their effects. More importantly, Bash skills build incrementally—you can start with simple command sequences and gradually incorporate more sophisticated programming constructs as your expertise grows.

The skills you develop while learning Bash scripting transfer readily to other areas of cybersecurity work. Understanding how to manipulate text files efficiently prepares you for log analysis tasks. Learning to work with network commands provides foundation knowledge for network security assessments. Mastering process management concepts helps with incident response and system forensics. These transferable skills make Bash proficiency a valuable investment that pays dividends across multiple cybersecurity domains.

Real-World Relevance: Where Bash Scripting Shines in Cybersecurity

The true value of Bash scripting in cybersecurity becomes evident when examining the specific scenarios and use cases where it provides clear advantages over alternative approaches. These real-world applications demonstrate why Bash has become an indispensable tool for security professionals working in diverse environments, from small startups to large enterprise networks. Understanding these applications helps illustrate not just what you can do with Bash, but when and why you should choose it over other available tools and techniques.

Incident Response and Digital Forensics

During security incidents, time is of the essence, and the ability to quickly gather, analyze, and correlate information from multiple sources can make the difference between containing a breach and experiencing a catastrophic compromise. Bash scripting excels in incident response scenarios because it enables rapid automation of evidence collection and analysis tasks that would otherwise require manual intervention at each step.

Consider a typical incident response scenario where you need to collect forensic evidence from multiple compromised systems. A well-crafted Bash script can automatically connect to each affected system, collect relevant log files, capture memory dumps, gather network connection information, and preserve file system metadata—all while maintaining proper chain of custody documentation. The script can also perform initial analysis on the collected data, identifying common indicators of compromise and highlighting anomalies that warrant further investigation.

The text-processing capabilities of Bash make it particularly valuable for log analysis during incident response. Security professionals often need to correlate events across multiple log sources, extract specific patterns from large datasets, and identify timeline relationships between different activities. Bash's integration with powerful text-processing tools like grep, sed, and awk enables sophisticated log analysis workflows that can process gigabytes of data efficiently, identifying needle-in-haystack indicators that might otherwise be missed.

Vulnerability Assessment and Penetration Testing

In vulnerability assessment and penetration testing contexts, Bash scripting provides the automation and customization capabilities necessary to conduct thorough, efficient security evaluations. Professional penetration testers routinely use Bash scripts to automate reconnaissance activities, coordinate multiple scanning tools, and process assessment results in ways that would be impractical to accomplish manually.

Network reconnaissance represents one area where Bash scripting provides value. A comprehensive network assessment might involve port scanning, service enumeration, version detection, and vulnerability identification across hundreds or thousands of network hosts. Bash scripts can orchestrate these activities, managing the execution of multiple tools while avoiding network congestion and detection by security systems. The scripts can also implement intelligent scheduling, adjusting scan intensity based on network conditions and target responsiveness.

The customization capabilities of Bash scripting become especially valuable when dealing with unique or complex target environments. While commercial vulnerability scanners provide broad coverage of common issues, they may miss environment-specific vulnerabilities or fail to adapt to unusual network configurations. Custom Bash scripts can implement specialized testing logic, combine multiple assessment techniques, and adapt their behavior based on discoveries made during the assessment process.

Security Monitoring and Alerting

Effective security monitoring requires continuous surveillance of system activities, network traffic, and application behavior—a task perfectly suited to Bash automation. Security operations centers (SOCs) routinely use Bash scripts to implement custom monitoring solutions that complement commercial security information and event management (SIEM) systems. These scripts can monitor specific indicators, process alerts from multiple sources, and implement automated response actions when predefined conditions are met.

Log monitoring represents a fundamental security monitoring application where Bash scripting provides significant value. While SIEM systems excel at processing and correlating large volumes of security events, they may not provide the flexibility needed to monitor highly specific indicators or implement custom analysis logic. Bash scripts can monitor log files in real-time, applying custom parsing logic to extract relevant information and triggering alerts when suspicious patterns are detected.

The real-time processing capabilities of Bash make it well-suited for implementing automated response actions based on security monitoring results. Scripts can automatically isolate compromised systems, update firewall rules to block malicious traffic, or escalate alerts to appropriate personnel based on the severity and nature of detected threats. This automation reduces response times and ensures that critical security events receive immediate attention, even outside normal business hours.

Compliance and Configuration Management

Regulatory compliance and security configuration management present ongoing challenges for organizations of all sizes. Bash scripting provides powerful tools for automating compliance assessments, implementing security hardening measures, and maintaining consistent security configurations across diverse system environments. These capabilities become increasingly important as organizations grow and as compliance requirements become more stringent and complex.

Security configuration assessments often require checking hundreds of individual settings across multiple systems, comparing current configurations against established baselines, and generating detailed reports documenting compliance status. Bash scripts can automate these assessments completely, connecting to target systems, collecting configuration information, performing compliance checks, and generating formatted reports without human intervention. This automation ensures that assessments are performed consistently and completely, reducing the risk of overlooking important configuration issues.

Configuration management represents another area where Bash scripting provides substantial value. Organizations need to maintain consistent security configurations across their infrastructure, implementing security hardening measures and ensuring that systems don't drift from established security baselines. Bash scripts can implement automated configuration management workflows that detect configuration drift, apply corrective measures, and document all changes for audit purposes.

Network Security and Traffic Analysis

Network security operations rely heavily on the analysis of network traffic patterns, connection logs, and communication metadata to identify potential threats and security violations. Bash scripting provides powerful tools for processing network data, correlating information from multiple sources, and implementing automated analysis workflows that can process large volumes of network information efficiently.

Network traffic analysis often involves processing captured packet data, extracting relevant metadata, and identifying patterns that might indicate malicious activity. Bash scripts can automate the processing of packet capture files, extract specific types of network communications, and correlate network activities with other security events. The scripts can also implement statistical analysis techniques to identify unusual traffic patterns that might indicate data exfiltration, command and control communications, or other suspicious activities.

Firewall log analysis represents another network security application where Bash scripting provides significant value. Organizations typically generate enormous volumes of firewall logs that must be analyzed to identify security violations, policy violations, and potential attack activities. Bash scripts can process these logs efficiently, extract relevant events, correlate activities across multiple time periods, and generate reports highlighting important security findings.

Automation of Security Tool Workflows

Modern cybersecurity operations rely on numerous specialized tools, each designed to address specific aspects of security management. While these tools are individually powerful, their true potential is often realized when they're integrated into comprehensive workflows that combine their capabilities. Bash scripting provides the glue that binds these tools together, creating automated workflows that leverage the strengths of multiple tools while minimizing the manual effort required to coordinate their operation.

Tool integration workflows might involve using Bash scripts to coordinate vulnerability scanners, patch management systems, and configuration management tools to implement comprehensive security maintenance processes. The scripts can schedule scans during appropriate maintenance windows, process scanner results to identify critical vulnerabilities, cross-reference findings with asset management databases, and automatically initiate patch deployment processes for systems that meet specific criteria.

The error handling and logging capabilities of Bash scripting become particularly important in automated tool workflows. When multiple tools are operating in sequence, failures in one component can cascade through the entire workflow, potentially causing data loss or incomplete operations. Well-designed Bash scripts implement comprehensive error handling that can detect failures, implement recovery procedures, and ensure that operators are notified when manual intervention is required.

What You'll Need: Setting Up a Safe Linux Environment for Practice

Creating an appropriate learning environment is crucial for developing practical Bash scripting skills safely and effectively. The environment you choose will directly impact your ability to experiment with different techniques, practice realistic scenarios, and build confidence in your scripting abilities without risking damage to production systems or sensitive data. This section provides comprehensive guidance for establishing a secure, isolated learning environment that supports all the activities covered in this book while maintaining appropriate safety boundaries.

Understanding the Importance of Isolation

Before diving into specific setup instructions, it's essential to understand why using an isolated practice environment is not just recommended but critical when learning cybersecurity-focused Bash scripting. Many of the techniques covered in this book involve activities that could be disruptive or potentially harmful if executed in the wrong context. Network scanning scripts, for example, might trigger security alerts or consume network bandwidth inappropriately if run against production networks. Similarly, system configuration scripts could modify critical settings or interfere with normal operations if executed on systems that others depend upon.

An isolated learning environment provides the freedom to experiment without consequences, allowing you to make mistakes, test different approaches, and develop understanding through hands-on exploration. This environment should be separate from any production systems, networks, or data, ensuring that your learning activities cannot inadvertently impact real operations or compromise sensitive information.

The isolation also serves a legal and ethical purpose. Many cybersecurity techniques, when applied inappropriately, could violate computer crime laws or organizational policies. By maintaining a clearly isolated learning environment, you ensure that all your activities are contained within systems that you own and control, eliminating any possibility of legal or ethical complications arising from your educational activities.

Virtual Machine Environments

Virtual machines represent the most practical and flexible approach for creating isolated Linux learning environments. Virtualization technology allows you to run complete Linux installations within your existing operating system, providing full functionality while maintaining complete isolation from your host system and network. This approach offers numerous advantages for cybersecurity learning, including the ability to create multiple different environments, easily reset systems to clean states, and safely test potentially disruptive techniques.

When selecting virtualization software for your learning environment, several options provide excellent capabilities for cybersecurity education. VMware Workstation Pro and VMware Fusion offer robust virtualization platforms with excellent performance and comprehensive networking options. VirtualBox provides a free alternative that includes most of the features needed for cybersecurity learning, though with somewhat lower performance than commercial alternatives. For users comfortable with command-line interfaces, QEMU/KVM offers powerful virtualization capabilities with fine-grained control over virtual machine configurations.

The virtual machine configuration should allocate sufficient resources to support realistic cybersecurity scenarios while avoiding excessive consumption of host system resources. A minimum of 2GB of RAM per virtual machine is recommended, with 4GB or more preferred for systems that will run multiple security tools simultaneously. Storage allocation should provide at least 20GB of disk space per virtual machine, allowing room for the operating system, security tools, practice datasets, and script development activities.

Network configuration represents a particularly important consideration for cybersecurity learning environments. Most virtualization platforms support multiple networking modes, including NAT, bridged, and host-only networking. For security learning purposes, host-only networking often provides the best balance of functionality and isolation, allowing virtual machines to communicate with each other and the host system while preventing any communication with external networks. This configuration supports realistic network-based learning scenarios while maintaining complete isolation from production networks.

Linux Distribution Selection

Choosing the appropriate Linux distribution for your learning environment significantly impacts your educational experience and the relevance of your practice activities to real-world cybersecurity scenarios. Different distributions offer varying levels of security tool integration, package availability, and community support, making some more suitable than others for cybersecurity education.

Kali Linux represents the most obvious choice for cybersecurity-focused learning environments. This Debian-based distribution includes an extensive collection of pre-installed security tools, optimized configurations for security testing activities, and excellent documentation for cybersecurity applications. Kali Linux provides immediate access to hundreds of security tools without requiring complex installation and configuration procedures, allowing you to focus on learning Bash scripting techniques rather than tool setup and management.

For learners who prefer to build their environments from more basic foundations, Ubuntu Server or CentOS provide excellent starting points that more closely resemble typical enterprise Linux deployments. These distributions require manual installation of security tools, providing valuable experience with package management and system configuration while building environments that closely mirror real-world scenarios. This approach requires more initial setup effort but provides deeper understanding of how security tools integrate with standard Linux distributions.

Specialized security distributions like Parrot Security OS or BlackArch Linux offer alternatives to Kali Linux with different tool collections and interface approaches. These distributions can provide valuable exposure to different tool ecosystems and configuration approaches, though they may require more learning overhead for users unfamiliar with their specific conventions and package management systems.

Essential Tools and Software Installation

Regardless of which Linux distribution you choose as your foundation, certain tools and software packages are essential for effective Bash scripting education in cybersecurity contexts. Installing and configuring these tools properly ensures that you can complete all the exercises and projects covered in this book while building familiarity with the security tool ecosystem that you'll encounter in professional cybersecurity environments.

Text editors represent fundamental tools for script development, and having appropriate editing software significantly impacts your productivity and learning effectiveness. While simple editors like nano provide basic functionality suitable for quick edits and system administration tasks, more sophisticated editors offer features that greatly enhance script development productivity. Vim or Emacs provide powerful editing capabilities with extensive customization options, though they require significant learning investment. For users preferring more familiar interfaces, Visual Studio Code or Sublime Text offer excellent balance of power and usability, with syntax highlighting, debugging integration, and extensive plugin ecosystems.

Version control software becomes increasingly important as your scripts grow more complex and as you begin developing larger automation projects. Git provides industry-standard version control capabilities that allow you to track changes to your scripts, experiment with different approaches without fear of losing working code and collaborate with others on script development projects. Installing Git and learning basic version control workflows early in your learning process establishes good development practices that will serve you well throughout your cybersecurity career.

Network analysis tools form a critical component of any cybersecurity learning environment. Wireshark provides comprehensive packet capture and analysis capabilities that complement many Bash scripting exercises involving network monitoring and traffic analysis. Nmap offers powerful network discovery and port scanning capabilities that integrate well with Bash automation scripts. tcpdump provides command-line packet capture functionality that works seamlessly within shell scripts for automated network monitoring applications.

Safe Practice Networks and Target Systems

Creating appropriate target systems and practice networks enhances the realism and educational value of your Bash scripting exercises while maintaining appropriate safety boundaries. These practice environments should provide realistic scenarios for testing your scripts without risking any damage to real systems or networks.

Vulnerable virtual machines designed specifically for security education provide excellent targets for practicing security-focused Bash scripting techniques. Deliberately vulnerable systems like Metasploitable, DVWA (Damn Vulnerable Web Application), and VulnHub virtual machines offer realistic security scenarios with known vulnerabilities that you can safely explore and exploit using your Bash scripts. These systems provide controlled environments where you can practice reconnaissance scripts, vulnerability assessment automation, and penetration testing techniques without legal or ethical concerns.

Creating your own practice networks using multiple virtual machines allows you to design scenarios that specifically support your learning objectives. A typical practice network might include several different operating systems, various network services, and different security configurations that provide diverse targets for your automation scripts. This approach requires more setup effort but provides complete control over the learning environment and ensures that practice scenarios align perfectly with your educational goals.

Documentation and logging systems help you track your learning progress and provide reference materials for future script development activities. Maintaining detailed notes about successful techniques, common problems and their solutions, and interesting discoveries encountered during your practice sessions creates a valuable personal reference that supports continued learning and professional development.

Security Considerations for Learning Environments

Even though you're learning environment is isolated from production systems, maintaining appropriate security practices protects your educational activities and builds good habits that transfer to professional cybersecurity work. These practices also ensure that your learning environment remains stable and reliable throughout your educational journey.

Regular backup procedures protect your investment in environment setup and script development against hardware failures, configuration errors, and other problems that might compromise your learning progress. Virtual machine snapshots provide convenient backup mechanisms that allow you to quickly restore known-good configurations when experiments go wrong or when you need to reset systems to clean states for new exercises.

Access control measures, even within your isolated learning environment, help build security awareness and establish good practices for handling sensitive information. Using strong passwords, implementing appropriate file permissions, and maintaining separate user accounts for different activities builds security consciousness that serves you well in professional environments.

Update management for your learning environment balances security considerations with educational stability requirements. While keeping systems updated with security patches is generally important, educational environments sometimes benefit from maintaining stable configurations that don't change unexpectedly. Developing a thoughtful approach to update management helps you understand the trade-offs involved in maintaining secure systems while preserving functional educational environments.

This comprehensive foundation provides everything needed to begin your journey into cybersecurity-focused Bash scripting. With an appropriate learning environment in place, you're ready to explore the powerful automation and security capabilities that make Bash scripting an essential skill for cybersecurity professionals. The following chapters will build upon this foundation, introducing progressively more sophisticated techniques while providing practical exercises that demonstrate real-world applications of your growing scripting expertise.

Chapter 1: The Bash Primer for Cyber Defenders

The journey into cybersecurity automation begins with mastering the fundamental building blocks of Bash scripting. While many cybersecurity professionals have some familiarity with basic command-line operations, developing true proficiency requires understanding not just what commands to execute, but how to combine them effectively, automate repetitive tasks, and build robust solutions that can handle the complex scenarios encountered in real-world security operations. This chapter establishes the essential foundation you need to progress from basic command execution to sophisticated automation scripting.

Understanding Bash fundamentals in a cybersecurity context requires more than memorizing syntax and command options. You need to develop an intuitive understanding of how the shell processes commands, how data flows between different tools and processes, and how to structure your scripts to handle the unpredictable conditions common in security work. The concepts covered in this chapter will serve as building blocks for every script you write throughout your cybersecurity career, making thorough mastery of these fundamentals essential for long-term success.

This chapter takes a practical approach to learning Bash fundamentals, focusing on concepts and techniques that directly support cybersecurity applications. Rather than covering every possible shell feature, we concentrate on the subset of functionality that provides the greatest value for security automation, monitoring, and analysis tasks. Each concept is introduced with cybersecurity-relevant examples and exercises that demonstrate immediate practical applications while building your understanding of underlying principles.

Navigating the Terminal Like a Pro

Effective terminal navigation forms the foundation of all advanced Bash scripting and cybersecurity automation. While basic navigation commands like cd and ls are familiar to most users, developing true proficiency requires understanding the full range of navigation techniques, shortcuts, and advanced features that enable efficient command-line work. Professional cybersecurity practitioners spend significant portions of their time working in terminal environments, making navigation efficiency a critical productivity factor that directly impacts their effectiveness in security operations.

Mastering Directory Structure and Path Navigation

Understanding Linux directory structure and path relationships is fundamental to effective terminal navigation and script development. The hierarchical file system structure used by Linux systems follows predictable patterns that, once understood, enable rapid navigation and efficient file management. For cybersecurity professionals, this understanding becomes particularly important when analyzing system compromises, investigating security incidents, or deploying security tools across different system configurations.

Absolute paths provide unambiguous references to file and directory locations, starting from the root directory and specifying the complete path to the target location. These paths are essential for script development because they ensure that your scripts can locate required files and directories regardless of the current working directory when the script executes. Understanding how to construct and use absolute paths effectively prevents many common scripting errors and makes your automation scripts more reliable and portable.

Relative paths offer efficiency advantages for navigation and scripting by specifying locations relative to the current working directory. Mastering relative path navigation enables rapid movement through directory structures and creates more maintainable scripts that can adapt to different deployment scenarios. The special directory references . (current directory) and .. (parent directory) provide powerful navigation shortcuts that become second nature with practice, enabling complex directory traversal operations with minimal typing.

The tilde expansion feature (~) provides convenient access to user home directories and represents one of the most frequently used navigation shortcuts in cybersecurity work. Understanding how tilde expansion works with different user contexts becomes particularly important when writing scripts that need to access user-specific configuration files, log directories, or data storage locations. The ability to reference home directories reliably across different user contexts is essential for creating portable automation scripts.

Command History and Efficiency Techniques

Command history functionality transforms the terminal from a simple command executor into a powerful productivity tool that learns from your work patterns and enables rapid command repetition and modification. The Bash history system maintains detailed records of previously executed commands, providing multiple mechanisms for accessing, searching, and reusing command sequences. For cybersecurity professionals who frequently execute complex command sequences, mastering history functionality can dramatically improve operational efficiency.

The history expansion system enables rapid recall and modification of previous commands using various syntax patterns. The !! operator repeats the previous command exactly, while !n executes the command at history position n, and !string executes the most recent command beginning with the specified string. These operators become particularly valuable during security investigations where you frequently need to repeat similar commands with slight modifications, such as running the same network scan against different target ranges or executing the same log analysis command against multiple files.

Reverse search functionality, accessed through the Ctrl+R key combination, provides interactive searching through command history that enables rapid location of previously executed commands based on partial matches. This functionality becomes invaluable when working with complex security tools that require lengthy command-line arguments or when trying to recall the exact syntax used for successful previous operations. Mastering reverse search techniques enables you to maintain detailed command histories without sacrificing access speed or convenience.

History configuration options allow customization of history behavior to support different work patterns and security requirements. The HISTSIZE variable controls the number of commands retained in memory during the current session, while HISTFILESIZE determines how many commands are saved to the history file for future sessions. For cybersecurity work, configuring appropriate history sizes ensures that you can access extensive command histories while managing storage and privacy considerations appropriately.

Advanced Navigation and File System Operations

Beyond basic navigation, professional terminal use requires familiarity with advanced techniques that enable efficient file system exploration, manipulation, and analysis. These techniques become particularly important in cybersecurity contexts where you frequently need to examine unfamiliar systems, locate specific files or configuration elements, and understand complex directory structures quickly and thoroughly.

The find command represents one of the most powerful tools for file system exploration and forms a cornerstone of many cybersecurity automation scripts. Understanding how to construct effective find commands enables rapid location of files based on various criteria including name patterns, modification times, permissions, and content characteristics. For security professionals, find commands frequently serve as the foundation for log analysis scripts, configuration auditing tools, and incident response automation.

Glob patterns and wildcard expansion provide efficient mechanisms for specifying multiple files or directories with similar characteristics. Understanding how bash expands patterns like *.log, backup_[0-9]*, and config.{conf,cfg,ini} enables creation of flexible commands that can adapt to different naming conventions and file organization schemes. These pattern matching capabilities become essential when developing scripts that need to process varying numbers of files with predictable naming patterns.

File system metadata examination using commands like stat, file, and lsattr provides detailed information about file characteristics that often prove crucial in security analysis contexts. Understanding how to interpret file timestamps, permissions, ownership, and special attributes enables more thorough security assessments and helps identify anomalies that might indicate security compromises or misconfigurations.

Terminal Customization and Productivity Enhancements

Customizing your terminal environment improves both productivity and effectiveness by adapting the interface to your specific work patterns and preferences. For cybersecurity professionals who spend extensive time in terminal environments, thoughtful customization can provide significant productivity improvements while reducing fatigue and improving focus during long analysis sessions.

Prompt customization enables you to display relevant information directly in your command prompt, reducing the need for frequent status checking commands and providing immediate context about your current environment. Security-focused prompt customizations might include current user and privilege level, system hostname, current directory, and git repository status. Understanding how to construct informative prompts helps maintain situational awareness during complex security operations.

Alias creation provides shortcuts for frequently used command sequences, reducing typing effort and minimizing syntax errors in commonly executed operations. Security professionals often benefit from aliases for common tasks like starting secure connections, launching monitoring tools, or executing standard analysis commands. Well-designed aliases improve both speed and consistency in command execution while reducing the cognitive load of remembering complex command syntax.

Tab completion configuration enhances command-line efficiency by providing intelligent completion suggestions for commands, file names, and command options. Understanding how to configure and extend tab completion functionality enables faster command entry and reduces syntax errors, particularly when working with complex security tools that have numerous command-line options and parameters.

Variables, Loops, and Conditionals: Scripting Essentials

The programming constructs available in Bash scripting transform the shell from a simple command executor into a powerful automation platform capable of implementing sophisticated logic and handling complex decision-making scenarios. For cybersecurity professionals, mastering these programming fundamentals enables the creation of intelligent automation scripts that can adapt to different conditions, process varying amounts of data, and implement complex analysis workflows without manual intervention.

Variable Declaration and Manipulation

Variables in Bash scripting serve as containers for storing and manipulating data throughout script execution, providing the foundation for creating dynamic, adaptable automation tools.

Understanding how to declare, assign, and manipulate variables effectively is essential for developing scripts that can handle the varying conditions and data types commonly encountered in cybersecurity operations. Unlike variables in many programming languages, Bash variables are fundamentally text-based, though they can represent numbers, file paths, command results, and complex data structures through appropriate handling techniques.

Variable assignment in Bash follows specific syntax rules that, while straightforward, require careful attention to spacing and quoting to avoid common pitfalls. The basic assignment format variable_name=value must not include spaces around the equals sign, a requirement that frequently trips up newcomers to shell scripting. Understanding when and how to use quotes during variable assignment becomes crucial when working with values that contain spaces, special characters, or shell metacharacters that might otherwise be interpreted incorrectly.

String manipulation capabilities in Bash provide powerful tools for processing and transforming text data, operations that are fundamental to many cybersecurity automation tasks. Parameter expansion techniques like ${variable#pattern} and ${variable%pattern} enable extraction of substrings, removal of prefixes and suffixes, and transformation of variable contents without requiring external tools. These built-in string manipulation capabilities improve script performance and reduce dependencies while providing the flexibility needed for processing log files, configuration data, and command output.

Environment variables provide a mechanism for sharing information between scripts and system processes, enabling creation of configurable automation tools that can adapt to different deployment environments. Understanding how to read environment variables, set them for child processes, and use them to control script behavior creates more flexible and maintainable automation solutions. In cybersecurity contexts, environment variables often store configuration information like target IP addresses, authentication credentials, and tool preferences that need to be accessible across multiple scripts and processes.

Array variables extend Bash's data handling capabilities by providing storage for multiple related values within a single variable structure. Understanding how to declare, populate, and iterate through arrays enables scripts to handle variable amounts of data efficiently, such as processing lists of target hosts, analyzing multiple log files, or managing collections of security tools. Array manipulation techniques become particularly valuable when developing scripts that need to process output from security tools that generate lists of findings or recommendations.

Control Flow with Conditionals

Conditional statements provide the decision-making capabilities that transform simple command sequences into intelligent automation tools capable of adapting their behavior based on current conditions, command results, and data analysis outcomes. For cybersecurity applications, conditional logic enables scripts to respond appropriately to different scenarios, handle error conditions gracefully, and implement complex analysis workflows that can branch based on security findings or system conditions.

The if statement forms the foundation of conditional logic in Bash scripting, providing the ability to execute different command sequences based on the results of test conditions. Understanding how to construct effective test conditions using command exit codes, file system tests, string comparisons, and numeric evaluations enables creation of scripts that can make intelligent decisions about how to proceed based on current circumstances. The syntax for if statements, while straightforward, requires careful attention to spacing and bracket usage to avoid syntax errors.

Test operators provide sophisticated condition evaluation capabilities that go far beyond simple true/false testing. File system test operators like -f (regular file), -d (directory), -r (readable), and -w (writable) enable scripts to verify system conditions before attempting operations, preventing errors and ensuring graceful handling of unexpected situations. String comparison operators allow scripts to analyze text data and make decisions based on pattern matches, content analysis, and data validation results.

Compound conditions using logical operators (&&, ||, and !) enable construction of complex conditional logic that can evaluate multiple criteria simultaneously. Understanding how to combine simple conditions into sophisticated decision-making logic enables creation of scripts that can handle the complex scenarios commonly encountered in cybersecurity operations, where multiple factors often need to be considered before determining the appropriate course of action.

The case statement provides an efficient mechanism for implementing multi-way branching logic when scripts need to respond differently to various possible values or conditions. This construct becomes particularly valuable when developing user interfaces for security tools, processing command-line arguments, or implementing different response strategies based on the types of security events or findings encountered during automated analysis operations.

Iteration with Loops

Loop constructs enable scripts to process multiple items, repeat operations until specific conditions are met, and implement monitoring functionality that continues indefinitely. For cybersecurity automation, loops are essential for processing lists of targets, monitoring system conditions over time, and implementing analysis workflows that need to examine large datasets or multiple system components systematically.

The for loop provides controlled iteration over predefined sets of values, making it ideal for processing lists of files, network hosts, or configuration items. Understanding how to construct for loops that iterate over command output, file contents, and array elements enables creation of scripts that can handle varying amounts of data efficiently. The ability to combine for loops with command substitution and variable expansion creates powerful processing workflows that can adapt to different data sources and formats.

The while loop enables conditional iteration that continues as long as specified conditions remain true, making it perfect for implementing monitoring scripts, processing input streams, and implementing retry logic for network operations. Understanding how to construct effective while loop conditions and manage loop termination prevents infinite loops while ensuring that monitoring and processing operations continue as long as necessary.

The until loop provides the inverse of while loop functionality, continuing iteration until a specified condition becomes true. This construct is particularly useful for implementing wait conditions, monitoring for the completion of background processes, and implementing timeout functionality in network-based operations where scripts need to wait for specific conditions to be satisfied.

Loop control statements like break and continue provide fine-grained control over loop execution, enabling scripts to skip inappropriate items, terminate loops early when objectives are achieved, and implement complex processing logic that can adapt to different conditions encountered during iteration. Understanding how to use these control statements effectively creates more efficient and robust automation scripts.

Advanced Scripting Constructs

Beyond basic programming constructs, Bash provides advanced features that enable creation of sophisticated automation tools capable of handling complex cybersecurity scenarios. These advanced constructs provide the flexibility and power needed to implement professional-quality automation solutions that can integrate with existing security infrastructure and adapt to changing operational requirements.

Function definition and invocation capabilities enable modular script development that promotes code reuse, simplifies maintenance, and improves script organization. Understanding how to define functions with appropriate parameter handling, return value management, and local variable scoping creates more maintainable and reliable scripts. For cybersecurity applications, functions often encapsulate common operations like network connectivity testing, log parsing, or report generation that are used across multiple scripts.

Command substitution techniques enable scripts to capture and use the output of other commands as variables or command arguments, creating powerful integration capabilities between different tools and processes. Understanding the differences between backtick syntax and the modern $() syntax, along with proper handling of command substitution in different contexts, enables creation of scripts that can effectively orchestrate complex tool chains and processing pipelines.

Process substitution provides advanced input/output redirection capabilities that enable scripts to treat command output as file inputs, enabling sophisticated data processing workflows that would otherwise require temporary files. This feature becomes particularly valuable when developing scripts that need to compare outputs from multiple tools, merge data from different sources, or implement complex analysis pipelines.

Error handling mechanisms including trap statements and exit code management enable creation of robust scripts that can handle unexpected conditions gracefully and provide appropriate feedback when problems occur. Understanding how to implement comprehensive error handling ensures that automation scripts behave predictably even when encountering unexpected system conditions or tool failures.

Permissions, Piping, and Redirection Basics

The Linux permission system and input/output redirection capabilities form critical components of effective Bash scripting for cybersecurity applications. Understanding how permissions work enables creation of secure scripts that can operate safely in multi-user environments while implementing appropriate access controls. Mastering piping and redirection techniques enables construction of powerful data processing workflows that can combine multiple tools and handle large datasets efficiently.

Understanding Linux File Permissions

The Linux permission system provides a sophisticated but comprehensible mechanism for controlling access to files, directories, and system resources. For cybersecurity professionals, understanding permissions is essential not only for creating secure scripts but also for analyzing system security, investigating potential compromises, and implementing appropriate access controls for automation tools and their associated data.

Basic permission concepts revolve around three types of access (read, write, execute) applied to three categories of users (owner, group, others). Understanding how these permissions interact enables prediction of what operations different users can perform on files and directories, which becomes crucial when developing scripts that need to operate in environments with multiple users or when analyzing systems for potential security vulnerabilities related to inappropriate file access.

Numeric permission representation provides a compact and precise method for specifying permission settings that proves particularly useful in scripting contexts. Understanding how the three-digit octal notation corresponds to permission bits enables efficient permission management and ensures that scripts can set appropriate access controls on files they create or modify. The ability to calculate and verify numeric permissions mentally becomes an invaluable skill during security assessments and incident response activities.

Special permission bits including the setuid, setgid, and sticky bits provide additional access control mechanisms that have significant security implications. Understanding how these special permissions work enables identification of potential security risks during system assessments and ensures that scripts implement appropriate security measures when creating files or executing privileged operations. The security implications of setuid scripts require careful consideration when developing automation tools that need elevated privileges.

Permission modification using chmod provides the primary mechanism for adjusting file and directory access controls. Understanding both symbolic and numeric chmod syntax enables efficient permission management in both interactive and scripted contexts. For security automation, the ability to set appropriate permissions on script files, log directories, and configuration files ensures that sensitive information remains protected while allowing necessary access for legitimate operations.

Directory permissions require special consideration because they control not only access to the directory itself but also the ability to list contents, create new files, and traverse through the directory structure. Understanding how directory permissions differ from file permissions enables creation of appropriate directory structures for security tools and ensures that scripts can access necessary resources while maintaining security boundaries.

Advanced Permission Concepts

Beyond basic permission management, several advanced concepts become important for cybersecurity applications where security and access control are paramount concerns. These advanced permission features provide additional layers of access control that can enhance the security posture of automation scripts and the systems they operate on.

Access Control Lists (ACLs) extend the basic permission model by providing fine-grained access control that can specify permissions for multiple users and groups beyond the basic owner/group/other model. Understanding how to view and modify ACLs enables creation of more sophisticated access control schemes for security tools and their associated data. While not all systems support ACLs, they are common in enterprise environments where detailed access control requirements exist.

File attributes provide additional file system features that can enhance security and system integrity. Understanding how to use commands like chattr and lsattr to manage file attributes like immutable, append-only, and no-dump settings provides additional tools for securing important files and implementing defense-in-depth strategies. These attributes can be particularly useful for protecting log files, configuration files, and other critical security-related data.

Ownership concepts including user and group ownership provide the foundation for implementing appropriate access controls in multi-user environments. Understanding how to manage file ownership using chown and chgrp commands enables creation of scripts that can operate safely in environments with multiple users while ensuring that sensitive files remain accessible only to appropriate personnel.

Mastering Input/Output Redirection

Input/output redirection forms the backbone of sophisticated Bash scripting by enabling precise control over where commands read their input and send their output. For cybersecurity applications, redirection enables creation of powerful data processing pipelines, automated logging systems, and complex analysis workflows that can handle large datasets efficiently while maintaining appropriate records of operations and results.

Standard stream concepts including stdin (standard input), stdout (standard output), and stderr (standard error) provide the foundation for understanding how commands receive input and produce output. Understanding how these streams work enables prediction of command behavior and effective design of data processing workflows. For security automation, the ability to separate normal output from error messages enables creation of scripts that can log operations appropriately while handling error conditions gracefully.

Output redirection using operators like >, >>, and 2> enables precise control over where command output is sent, allowing scripts to create log files, save analysis results, and manage temporary data efficiently. Understanding the differences between overwriting (>) and appending (>>) output enables creation of scripts that can maintain persistent logs while avoiding accidental data loss. The ability to redirect error output separately from normal output provides sophisticated error handling and logging capabilities.

Input redirection using the < operator enables scripts to read data from files rather than requiring interactive input, making automation possible for commands that normally expect user interaction. Understanding how to use input redirection effectively enables creation of scripts that can process batch operations and handle large datasets without manual intervention.

Here documents and here strings provide advanced input redirection techniques that enable scripts to provide multi-line input to commands or create temporary input data on-the-fly. These techniques become particularly useful when developing scripts that need to interact with tools that expect specific input formats or when creating template-based output generation systems.

Pipe Operations and Command Chaining

Pipe operations represent one of the most powerful features of the Unix command-line environment, enabling creation of sophisticated data processing workflows by connecting the output of one command directly to the input of another. For cybersecurity applications, pipes enable construction of complex analysis workflows that can process large datasets, filter information based on specific criteria and transform data through multiple processing stages.

Basic piping concepts involve connecting commands using the pipe operator (|) to create linear processing workflows where data flows from one command to the next in sequence. Understanding how pipes work enables prediction of data flow through command chains and effective design of processing workflows that can accomplish complex tasks through the combination of simple tools. The Unix philosophy of creating simple tools that do one thing well finds its full expression in sophisticated pipe-based workflows.

Multi-stage processing pipelines enable transformation of raw data through multiple processing steps to produce refined, analyzed results. Understanding how to design effective pipelines requires consideration of data formats, processing requirements, and performance characteristics of different tools. For security applications, pipelines frequently combine tools like grep, awk, sed, and sort to extract, filter, and analyze security-related information from log files and system output.

Error handling in pipelines requires understanding how error conditions propagate through pipe chains and how to implement appropriate error detection and recovery mechanisms. The pipefail option causes pipelines to fail if any component fails, providing more robust error detection than the default behavior. Understanding how to implement effective error handling in pipelines ensures that automation scripts behave predictably even when encountering unexpected conditions.

Process substitution provides advanced piping capabilities that enable commands to receive input from multiple sources or send output to multiple destinations simultaneously. Understanding how to use process substitution effectively enables creation of sophisticated data processing workflows that can compare outputs from multiple sources, merge data streams, or implement complex analysis logic that would otherwise require temporary files.

Text Processing and Data Manipulation

Text processing capabilities form a core component of cybersecurity automation, enabling analysis of log files, configuration data, command output, and other text-based information sources. Understanding how to effectively process and manipulate text data using command-line tools enables creation of powerful analysis scripts that can extract meaningful information from large datasets and identify patterns that might indicate security issues.

The grep command family provides powerful pattern matching capabilities that enable extraction of specific information from large text files. Understanding how to construct effective regular expressions and use advanced grep options enables creation of sophisticated filtering and search operations. For cybersecurity applications, grep operations frequently serve as the foundation for log analysis, configuration auditing, and threat hunting activities.

Stream editing with sed enables sophisticated text transformation operations that can modify, replace, and restructure text data as it flows through processing pipelines. Understanding sed's command syntax and addressing mechanisms enables creation of scripts that can clean data, standardize formats, and extract specific information from structured text sources. The ability to perform complex text transformations within pipelines eliminates the need for temporary files while maintaining processing efficiency.

Pattern scanning and processing with awk provides sophisticated data extraction and analysis capabilities that bridge the gap between simple text filtering and full programming languages. Understanding awk's programming model enables creation of complex data analysis operations that can process structured text data, perform calculations, and generate formatted reports. For cybersecurity applications, awk frequently serves as the foundation for log analysis scripts and data processing workflows.

Text sorting and uniqueness operations using sort and uniq enable organization and deduplication of data sets, operations that are fundamental to many security analysis workflows. Understanding how to use these tools effectively enables creation of scripts that can process large datasets efficiently while producing organized, meaningful results. The combination of sorting and uniqueness operations provides powerful capabilities for analyzing patterns in security data.

Writing Your First Automated Script

Creating your first automation script represents the culmination of fundamental Bash learning and the beginning of practical cybersecurity automation development. This section guides you through the process of designing, implementing, and testing a complete automation script that demonstrates essential scripting concepts while solving a real cybersecurity problem. The script development process covered here establishes patterns and practices that will serve as templates for more sophisticated automation projects throughout your cybersecurity career.

Planning and Design Considerations

Effective script development begins with careful planning and design that considers the problem being solved, the environment where the script will operate, and the requirements for reliability, maintainability, and security. For cybersecurity applications, the planning phase must also consider the potential security implications of the script itself, ensuring that automation tools do not introduce new vulnerabilities or create inappropriate access to sensitive information.

Problem definition provides the foundation for all subsequent design decisions and should clearly articulate what the script needs to accomplish, what inputs it will process, and what outputs it should produce. For our first script example, we'll create a network connectivity checker that can test connectivity to multiple hosts and generate a summary report of results. This problem represents a common cybersecurity task that demonstrates essential scripting concepts while producing genuinely useful results.

Input and output specification defines how the script will receive configuration information and how it will present results to users. Understanding how to design clear, consistent interfaces for your scripts ensures that they integrate well with other tools and can be used effectively by other team members. Our connectivity checker will accept a list of hostnames or IP addresses as input and produce both detailed per-host results and a summary report as output.

Error handling strategy development ensures that scripts behave predictably when encountering unexpected conditions or system problems. For cybersecurity applications, robust error handling is particularly important because security tools often operate in unpredictable environments where network conditions, system configurations, and target availability can vary significantly. Our script will implement comprehensive error handling that provides clear feedback about problems while continuing to process remaining targets when possible.

Security considerations for script development include protecting sensitive information, implementing appropriate access controls, and ensuring that the script itself does not create security vulnerabilities. Understanding how to develop scripts that operate securely in multi-user environments while handling potentially sensitive information like network configurations and connectivity results establishes good security practices from the beginning of your scripting journey.

Script Structure and Organization

Well-organized scripts follow predictable patterns that make them easier to understand, maintain, and debug. Establishing good organizational practices from the beginning of your scripting experience creates habits that will serve you well as your scripts become more complex and as you begin working on team-based automation projects.

Script headers provide essential documentation that explains the script's purpose, requirements, and usage patterns. A comprehensive header should include the script name, description, author information, version history, and usage examples. For cybersecurity scripts, headers should also document any security considerations, required privileges, and potential impact on systems or networks. Our connectivity checker will include a detailed header that serves as a template for future script development.

Variable declaration and initialization sections establish the script's configuration and provide clear documentation of customizable parameters. Organizing variable declarations at the beginning of the script makes it easy to modify script behavior without understanding implementation details. Our example script will demonstrate how to organize variables logically and provide clear documentation of their purposes and acceptable values.

Function organization enables modular script development that promotes code reuse and simplifies maintenance. Understanding how to break complex operations into logical functions creates more readable and maintainable scripts while enabling reuse of common operations across multiple scripts. Our connectivity checker will demonstrate effective function organization for common operations like connectivity testing, result formatting, and error handling.

Main script logic organization provides the overall flow control that coordinates different script components and implements the primary processing workflow. Understanding how to structure main script logic clearly enables creation of scripts that are easy to follow and debug while maintaining appropriate separation between different functional areas.

Implementation of Core Functionality

The implementation phase translates design specifications into working code that demonstrates essential Bash scripting concepts while solving the defined problem. Our network connectivity checker will implement functionality for reading target lists, testing connectivity to multiple hosts, collecting results, and generating summary reports.

Target list processing demonstrates file input handling and data validation techniques that are fundamental to many cybersecurity automation scripts. Our script will read target hosts from a file, validate the format of each entry, and handle various input formats including hostnames, IP addresses, and port specifications. Understanding how to process input files robustly enables creation of scripts that can handle real-world data with inconsistent formatting and quality.

Connectivity testing implementation demonstrates network operations and external command integration that are common in cybersecurity scripts. Our script will use ping and netcat commands to test different types of connectivity while capturing and interpreting results appropriately. Understanding how to integrate external tools effectively enables creation of scripts that leverage the full ecosystem of security tools available on Linux systems.

Result collection and processing demonstrates data structure management and results aggregation techniques that enable scripts to provide meaningful summary information. Our script will collect detailed results from individual connectivity tests and maintain summary statistics that provide overall assessment of network connectivity status. Understanding how to manage complex data structures in Bash enables creation of scripts that can handle sophisticated analysis and reporting requirements.

Progress reporting and user feedback implementation demonstrates user interface design principles that make scripts more usable and professional. Our script will provide real-time progress updates during execution and present results in clear, organized formats that enable rapid assessment of connectivity status. Understanding how to design effective user interfaces for command-line tools improves script usability and adoption.

Testing and Validation Procedures

Thorough testing ensures that scripts work correctly under various conditions and handle error cases appropriately. For cybersecurity applications, comprehensive testing is particularly important because automation scripts often operate in critical environments where failures can have significant consequences. Establishing good testing practices from the beginning of your scripting experience creates habits that will serve you well throughout your career.

Unit testing approaches for shell scripts involve testing individual functions and components in isolation to ensure that they work correctly under various input conditions. Understanding how to create effective test cases for shell script components enables identification of problems early in the development process while ensuring that individual components work reliably. Our connectivity checker will demonstrate testing approaches for input validation, connectivity testing, and result processing functions.

Integration testing validates that different script components work together correctly and that the overall script workflow produces expected results. Understanding how to design effective integration tests ensures that scripts work correctly as complete systems while identifying interaction problems between different components. Integration testing becomes particularly important for scripts that coordinate multiple external tools or process complex data workflows.

Error condition testing ensures that scripts handle unexpected conditions gracefully and provide appropriate feedback when problems occur. Understanding how to simulate various error conditions and validate script responses enables creation of robust automation tools that behave predictably even when encountering system problems or unexpected input. Our example script will demonstrate error handling for network connectivity problems, invalid input data, and system resource issues.

Performance testing evaluates script efficiency and resource usage under realistic operating conditions. Understanding how to assess script performance enables optimization of processing workflows and ensures that automation tools can handle expected workloads without consuming excessive system resources. For network-based scripts like our connectivity checker, performance testing must consider both processing efficiency and network resource usage.

Documentation and Maintenance Practices

Effective documentation ensures that scripts remain usable and maintainable over time, even as system environments change, and team membership evolves. For cybersecurity applications, good documentation also supports incident response activities where team members may need to understand and modify scripts quickly under pressure.

Inline documentation using comments explains complex logic, documents important assumptions, and provides context for future maintainers. Understanding how to write effective comments that explain not just what the script does but why it takes specific approaches enables creation of scripts that can be maintained and modified by other team members. Our example script demonstrates commenting practices that provide appropriate detail without cluttering the code.

Usage documentation explains how to use the script effectively, including command-line options, input file formats, and interpretation of results. Understanding how to create clear, comprehensive usage documentation enables other team members to adopt and use your scripts effectively while reducing support burden. Good usage documentation should include examples that demonstrate common use cases and explain how to interpret script output.

Maintenance procedures documentation explains how to modify, extend, and troubleshoot the script when requirements change, or problems are discovered. Understanding how to document maintenance procedures enables scripts to evolve effectively over time while maintaining reliability and functionality. For cybersecurity scripts, maintenance documentation should also explain security considerations and testing procedures for validating modifications.

Version control practices ensure that script changes are tracked appropriately and that previous versions can be recovered when needed. Understanding how to use version control effectively for script development enables collaboration with team members while providing recovery mechanisms when modifications introduce problems. Effective version control practices become increasingly important as scripts grow more complex and as they become integrated into critical operational workflows.

Conclusion

This chapter has established the fundamental building blocks necessary for effective Bash scripting in cybersecurity contexts. From mastering terminal navigation and understanding the intricacies of file permissions to implementing sophisticated control flow logic and creating your first automation script, you've developed a solid foundation that will support increasingly complex automation projects throughout your cybersecurity career.

The concepts covered in this chapter—variables, loops, conditionals, permissions, piping, and redirection—form the core vocabulary of Bash scripting that you'll use in every subsequent chapter. More importantly, you've learned not just the syntax of these features but how to apply them effectively in cybersecurity scenarios where reliability, security, and efficiency are paramount concerns. The practical approach taken throughout this chapter ensures that you understand not only what these features do, but when and why to use them in real-world security automation contexts.

The network connectivity checker script developed in the final section demonstrates how these fundamental concepts combine to create useful automation tools that solve genuine cybersecurity problems. This script serves as a template for future development projects while illustrating essential practices for script planning, implementation, testing, and documentation. The patterns and practices demonstrated in this example will serve you well as you progress to more sophisticated automation projects in subsequent chapters.

Moving forward, the skills developed in this chapter will enable you to tackle increasingly complex cybersecurity automation challenges. The solid foundation in Bash fundamentals you've established provides the confidence and competence necessary to explore advanced topics like network scanning automation, log analysis workflows, incident response tools, and security monitoring systems. Each new technique you learn will build upon the fundamental concepts mastered in this chapter, creating a comprehensive toolkit for cybersecurity automation and analysis.

The journey from basic command execution to sophisticated automation scripting represents a significant step in your development as a cybersecurity professional. The investment you've made in understanding these fundamental concepts will pay dividends throughout your career as you encounter new challenges that can be solved through effective automation. With these fundamentals firmly established, you're ready to explore the more specialized cybersecurity applications that make Bash scripting an indispensable tool for modern security operations.

Chapter 2: Automate Reconnaissance and Scanning

Reconnaissance forms the foundation of virtually every cybersecurity engagement, from penetration testing and vulnerability assessments to incident response and threat hunting. The ability to systematically gather information about target systems, networks, and organizations determines the success of subsequent security activities. While manual reconnaissance can provide detailed insights, the scale and complexity of modern network environments demand automated approaches that can efficiently process large amounts of data while maintaining thoroughness and accuracy.

Bash scripting provides an ideal platform for automating reconnaissance activities because of its seamless integration with the extensive ecosystem of reconnaissance tools available on Linux systems. Unlike GUI-based solutions that limit flexibility and automation potential, command-line tools controlled through Bash scripts can be orchestrated into sophisticated workflows that adapt to different scenarios, process varying amounts of data, and generate comprehensive reports that support decision-making throughout the security assessment process.

This chapter focuses on building practical automation skills for the most common reconnaissance and scanning activities encountered in cybersecurity work. Rather than simply explaining how individual tools work, we'll explore how to combine multiple tools through intelligent automation, parse and correlate results from different sources, and create reusable toolkits that can adapt to various engagement requirements. The techniques covered here form the foundation for more advanced automation projects while providing immediate value for day-to-day security operations.

The progression through this chapter builds from automating individual tools to creating comprehensive reconnaissance frameworks that demonstrate professional-level automation capabilities. Each section introduces new concepts while reinforcing fundamental scripting principles covered in the previous chapter, ensuring that your automation skills develop systematically while maintaining focus on practical cybersecurity applications.

Automating Nmap and Parsing Results

Network mapping with Nmap represents one of the most fundamental reconnaissance activities in cybersecurity, providing essential information about network topology, host availability, service configurations, and potential vulnerabilities. While Nmap's extensive feature set makes it incredibly powerful, the tool's complexity and the volume of data it can generate make automation essential for efficient use in professional environments. Effective Nmap automation requires understanding not only the tool's capabilities but also how to structure scans appropriately, process results efficiently and extract meaningful insights from large datasets.

Understanding Nmap Fundamentals for Automation

Nmap's scanning capabilities extend far beyond simple port scanning, encompassing host discovery, service version detection, operating system fingerprinting, and vulnerability assessment through its scripting engine. Understanding how these different scan types work and when to use them appropriately enables creation of automation scripts that can adapt their scanning approach based on engagement requirements, target characteristics, and time constraints.

Host discovery techniques form the foundation of network reconnaissance by identifying which systems are available and responsive within target network ranges. Nmap provides multiple host discovery methods including ICMP echo requests, TCP SYN scans to common ports, UDP probes, and ARP requests for local network segments. Understanding the advantages and limitations of different discovery methods enables creation of automation scripts that can adapt their approach based on network characteristics and security controls that might block certain types of probes.

The selection of appropriate discovery methods becomes particularly important in automated scenarios where scripts must operate efficiently across diverse network environments. Different networks may block ICMP traffic, filter specific TCP ports, or implement other security measures that affect the reliability of various discovery techniques. Effective automation scripts implement multiple discovery methods and can fall back to alternative approaches when primary methods fail to produce reliable results.

Port scanning strategies require careful consideration of scan timing, target selection, and result interpretation to balance thoroughness with efficiency and stealth requirements. Nmap's timing templates provide predefined configurations that optimize scan behavior for different scenarios, from very slow stealth scans that avoid detection to aggressive scans that prioritize speed over stealth. Understanding how these timing templates affect scan behavior enables creation of automation scripts that can adjust their approach based on engagement parameters and target sensitivity.

Service version detection adds significant value to port scanning by identifying the specific software versions running on discovered services, information that proves crucial for vulnerability assessment and attack planning. However, version detection significantly increases scan time and network traffic, making it important to use this capability judiciously in automated scenarios. Effective automation scripts implement intelligent service selection that focuses version detection efforts on services most likely to yield valuable information.

Command Line Automation Strategies

Automating Nmap effectively requires understanding how to construct appropriate command lines that produce consistent, parseable results while adapting to different scanning scenarios. The tool's extensive command-line options provide tremendous flexibility, but this flexibility also creates complexity when designing automation scripts that must handle various target types, scan requirements, and output formats.

Output format selection proves crucial for automation because different output formats provide different advantages for parsing and analysis. Nmap's XML output format provides the most comprehensive and structured results, making it ideal for automated processing, while the grepable format offers simpler parsing for basic automation needs. Understanding the trade-offs between different output formats enables selection of appropriate formats for different automation scenarios.

The XML output format deserves particular attention because it provides complete scan results in a structured format that can be processed reliably by automated tools. XML output includes detailed timing information, scan statistics, host status data, port information, service details, and script results in a hierarchical structure that preserves all relationships between different data elements. This comprehensive structure makes XML output ideal for automation scripts that need to perform complex analysis or correlation of scan results.

Target specification strategies affect both scan efficiency and result quality, making it important to understand how to specify targets appropriately for different automation scenarios. Nmap supports multiple target specification methods including individual IP addresses, CIDR network ranges, hostname resolution, and input from files. Understanding how to combine these methods effectively enables creation of flexible automation scripts that can handle diverse target requirements while optimizing scan efficiency.

Scan timing and performance optimization become critical factors when automating Nmap for large-scale reconnaissance operations. The tool's default timing settings work well for interactive use but may not be optimal for automated scenarios where scan time, network impact, and detection avoidance requirements differ from typical manual usage. Understanding how to adjust timing parameters, parallelization settings, and resource usage limits enables creation of automation scripts that can operate efficiently within various operational constraints.

Result Parsing and Data Extraction

Processing Nmap results effectively requires understanding the structure and content of different output formats while implementing robust parsing logic that can handle the variations and edge cases encountered in real-world scanning scenarios. The volume of data generated by comprehensive network scans makes manual analysis impractical, necessitating automated approaches that can extract relevant information, identify patterns, and highlight findings that require attention.

XML parsing techniques provide the most robust approach for processing comprehensive Nmap results because the XML format preserves all scan data in a structured format that can be processed reliably. Understanding how to navigate XML document structure using command-line tools like xmllint and programming constructs enables extraction of specific information while maintaining context about scan conditions and result reliability.

The hierarchical structure of Nmap XML output requires understanding the relationships between different data elements to extract information correctly. Host elements contain port and service information, script results reference specific services or hosts, and timing information provides context about scan reliability and network conditions. Understanding these relationships enables creation of parsing logic that can extract relevant information while maintaining appropriate context.

Regular expression techniques prove valuable for parsing text-based Nmap output formats and extracting specific information from XML content. Understanding how to construct effective regular expressions for matching IP addresses, port numbers, service names, and other common data elements enables creation of flexible parsing logic that can adapt to different output formats and extract relevant information reliably.

Data normalization and standardization become important when processing results from multiple scans or combining information from different sources. Nmap output may include variations in service names, port state descriptions, and other textual elements that require normalization for effective analysis and correlation. Understanding how to implement consistent data normalization enables creation of automation scripts that produce reliable, comparable results across different scanning scenarios.

Error handling for parsing operations must account for the various ways that Nmap scans can produce incomplete or inconsistent results. Network timeouts, filtered ports, and scan interruptions can create XML output that deviates from expected structures or contains incomplete information. Robust parsing logic implements appropriate error handling that can process partial results while identifying cases where scan reliability may be compromised.

Advanced Nmap Automation Techniques

Beyond basic scan automation, advanced techniques enable creation of sophisticated reconnaissance workflows that adapt their behavior based on initial findings, implement intelligent target selection, and coordinate multiple scanning approaches to gather comprehensive information about target environments. These advanced approaches demonstrate the full potential of Bash automation for complex cybersecurity tasks.

Adaptive scanning strategies adjust scan parameters based on initial reconnaissance results, enabling more efficient and targeted information gathering. An initial host discovery scan might identify active systems that warrant more detailed port scanning, while service detection results could trigger vulnerability-specific script execution. Understanding how to implement adaptive logic enables creation of automation scripts that optimize their approach based on discovered target characteristics.

The implementation of adaptive scanning requires careful design of decision logic that can evaluate scan results and determine appropriate follow-up actions. This might involve analyzing service detection results to identify potentially vulnerable services, assessing port scan results to determine appropriate script selections, or evaluating network response times to adjust scan timing parameters. Effective adaptive logic balances thoroughness with efficiency while maintaining appropriate bounds on scan scope and duration.

Distributed scanning techniques enable coordination of multiple Nmap instances to accelerate reconnaissance of large network ranges while managing resource consumption and detection risk. Understanding how to partition target ranges appropriately and coordinate multiple scanning processes enables creation of automation scripts that can scale to handle enterprise-sized networks efficiently.

The coordination of distributed scanning requires careful management of target allocation, result collection, and resource usage to ensure that scanning operations complete efficiently without overwhelming network resources or triggering security controls. Effective distributed scanning implementations include mechanisms for monitoring scan progress, handling failures gracefully, and consolidating results from multiple scanning processes.

Integration with vulnerability databases enables automation scripts to correlate service detection results with known vulnerabilities, providing immediate assessment of potential security risks. Understanding how to access and query vulnerability databases programmatically enables creation of reconnaissance workflows that provide actionable security intelligence rather than just raw scan data.

Script engine automation leverages Nmap's extensive scripting capabilities to gather specialized information about discovered services and systems. The Nmap Scripting Engine (NSE) includes hundreds of scripts for vulnerability detection, service enumeration, and security assessment that can be invoked selectively based on scan results. Understanding how to automate script selection and execution enables creation of comprehensive reconnaissance workflows that adapt their approach based on discovered target characteristics.

Bash with Whois, Dig, and Nslookup

Domain name system (DNS) analysis and domain registration research form critical components of comprehensive reconnaissance that provide valuable intelligence about target organizations, network infrastructure, and potential attack vectors. While individual DNS queries and whois lookups provide useful information, the true value of this reconnaissance approach emerges when these activities are automated, and their results are correlated to build comprehensive intelligence profiles about target environments.

Understanding DNS Reconnaissance Fundamentals

DNS reconnaissance provides multiple avenues for gathering intelligence about target organizations and their network infrastructure. The hierarchical nature of the DNS system creates multiple opportunities for information gathering, from analyzing domain registration data and nameserver configurations to enumerating subdomains and analyzing DNS record types that reveal infrastructure details.

Domain name resolution provides the foundation for understanding how target organizations structure their online presence and can reveal information about internal network architecture, third-party service usage, and business relationships. Understanding how DNS resolution works enables creation of automation scripts that can systematically explore domain hierarchies and identify resources that might not be immediately obvious through direct reconnaissance.

The relationship between domain names and IP addresses often reveals patterns that indicate network architecture, hosting arrangements, and organizational structure. Organizations frequently use predictable naming conventions for their systems, create DNS records that reflect internal network topology, and establish relationships between domains that reveal business operations and partnerships. Understanding how to analyze these relationships systematically enables extraction of valuable intelligence from DNS data.

DNS record types provide different categories of information that serve distinct reconnaissance purposes. A records reveal IP address mappings, MX records indicate email infrastructure, NS records show nameserver relationships, and TXT records often contain policy information and service configurations. Understanding how different record types contribute to reconnaissance enables creation of comprehensive DNS analysis workflows that gather all available information systematically.

Reverse DNS analysis provides an additional perspective on target infrastructure by revealing hostname information associated with known IP addresses. This technique often discovers systems and services that are not directly referenced by forward DNS queries, particularly internal systems that may be accessible from certain network positions. Understanding how to implement systematic reverse DNS analysis enables more comprehensive reconnaissance of target network ranges.

Whois Database Analysis and Automation

Whois databases contain registration information about domains and IP address allocations that provide valuable intelligence about target organizations, their network resources, and business relationships. While basic whois queries are straightforward, effective automation requires understanding how different whois servers work, how to handle varying data formats, and how to extract meaningful intelligence from registration data.

Domain registration analysis reveals information about target organizations including registration dates, contact information, nameserver configurations, and domain status that can provide insights into organizational structure and operational practices. Understanding how to parse whois data systematically enables extraction of intelligence that supports other reconnaissance activities and provides context for discovered network resources.

Registration data parsing requires handling the significant variations in whois output formats between different registrars and registration databases. Different whois servers use varying field names, date formats, and data organization schemes that require flexible parsing logic to handle reliably. Understanding how to implement robust parsing that can adapt to different whois formats enables creation of automation scripts that work reliably across diverse target domains.

Historical registration analysis provides temporal context about domain ownership changes, infrastructure modifications, and organizational evolution that can reveal business relationships and operational patterns. While current whois data provides a snapshot of present registration status, historical analysis can reveal patterns of domain acquisition, infrastructure changes, and ownership transfers that provide additional intelligence about target organizations.

Contact information analysis from whois data can reveal organizational structure, key personnel, and business relationships that support social engineering activities and provide context for other reconnaissance findings. However, contact information analysis must be conducted carefully to respect privacy considerations and legal boundaries while extracting intelligence that supports legitimate security assessment activities.

IP address allocation analysis through whois databases reveals information about network ownership, geographic distribution, and organizational relationships that provide context for network reconnaissance activities. Understanding how IP address allocations are documented in whois databases enables creation of automation scripts that can identify network ranges associated with target organizations and their business partners.

DNS Query Automation and Analysis

Automating DNS queries effectively requires understanding how to construct appropriate query sequences, handle different response types, and implement robust error handling for network operations that may encounter timeouts, failures, or inconsistent responses. The distributed nature of the DNS system creates multiple opportunities for gathering information while also introducing complexity in terms of query reliability and response consistency.

Systematic subdomain enumeration represents one of the most valuable DNS reconnaissance techniques, revealing systems and services that might not be discovered through other means. Understanding how to implement efficient subdomain enumeration requires balancing thoroughness with query rate limits and implementing appropriate techniques for handling large domain namespaces.

Subdomain enumeration strategies range from brute-force approaches that test common subdomain names to more sophisticated techniques that leverage DNS zone transfers, certificate transparency logs, and search engine results. Understanding the advantages and limitations of different enumeration approaches enables creation of automation scripts that can adapt their strategy based on target characteristics and available time.

Dictionary-based enumeration uses predefined lists of common subdomain names to discover systems systematically. This approach provides good coverage of typical subdomain naming patterns while maintaining reasonable query volumes and execution times. Understanding how to select and customize subdomain dictionaries enables creation of enumeration scripts that balance comprehensiveness with efficiency.

Recursive enumeration builds upon initial subdomain discoveries by testing additional naming patterns based on discovered subdomains. This technique often reveals additional systems that follow similar naming conventions or organizational patterns. Understanding how to implement recursive enumeration safely prevents infinite loops while maximizing discovery potential.

DNS record type analysis involves querying for different types of DNS records to gather comprehensive information about discovered domains and systems. Different record types provide different categories of information, and systematic analysis of all relevant record types ensures that automation scripts gather all available intelligence about target systems.

Zone transfer attempts represent a specialized DNS reconnaissance technique that can reveal comprehensive information about domain configurations when successful. While most properly configured DNS servers prevent unauthorized zone transfers, testing for this vulnerability provides valuable information when successful and helps assess DNS security configurations.

Advanced DNS Intelligence Gathering

Beyond basic DNS queries and subdomain enumeration, advanced techniques enable gathering of more sophisticated intelligence that provides deeper insights into target infrastructure and operations. These techniques often involve correlating information from multiple sources and implementing analysis workflows that identify patterns and relationships in DNS data.

DNS cache poisoning detection and analysis can reveal information about DNS infrastructure security and provide insights into how target organizations implement DNS security controls. Understanding how to test for various DNS security configurations enables assessment of potential attack vectors while providing intelligence about target security posture.

Certificate transparency log analysis provides an alternative source of subdomain information that often reveals systems not discoverable through traditional enumeration techniques. Certificate transparency logs contain records of SSL certificates issued for domains, including subdomains, providing a comprehensive view of an organization's SSL-enabled infrastructure.

Understanding how to query certificate transparency logs programmatically enables creation of automation scripts that can discover SSL-enabled systems without generating DNS queries that might be detected by monitoring systems. This approach often reveals systems that use non-standard subdomain naming patterns or that are not referenced by other discovery methods.

DNS monitoring and change detection enables identification of infrastructure modifications that might indicate new systems, service changes, or security improvements. Understanding how to implement systematic DNS monitoring enables creation of automation scripts that can track infrastructure evolution over time and identify opportunities or threats associated with infrastructure changes.

Passive DNS analysis leverages historical DNS resolution data to understand how target infrastructure has evolved over time and to identify relationships between different domains and IP addresses. While passive DNS data requires access to specialized databases, understanding how to analyze this information provides valuable historical context for reconnaissance activities.

Geographic DNS analysis examines how DNS resolution varies based on query location, revealing information about content delivery networks, geographic load balancing, and regional infrastructure distribution. Understanding how to implement geographic DNS analysis enables assessment of target infrastructure distribution and identification of regional access points that might present different attack surfaces.

Building a Script to Scan Open Ports and Save Logs

Creating a comprehensive port scanning script that can handle various scanning scenarios while maintaining detailed logs represents a practical application of Bash automation principles that demonstrates professional-level scripting capabilities. This script development project integrates multiple concepts from previous sections while introducing new techniques for log management, result analysis, and user interface design.

Script Architecture and Design Principles

Effective port scanning scripts require careful architectural design that balances functionality, usability, and maintainability while implementing appropriate security measures and logging capabilities. The architecture decisions made during initial script design significantly impact the script's ability to handle diverse scanning scenarios and evolve to meet changing requirements over time.

Modular design principles enable creation of scripts that can be easily understood, modified, and extended without requiring comprehensive rewrites. Understanding how to decompose complex scanning operations into logical modules enables creation of scripts that separate concerns appropriately while maintaining clear interfaces between different functional components.

The separation of scanning logic from result processing enables independent optimization of different script components while facilitating testing and validation of individual functions. This modular approach also enables reuse of scanning components in other scripts and simplifies maintenance when scanning requirements or target environments change.

Configuration management design enables scripts to adapt to different scanning scenarios without requiring code modifications. Understanding how to implement flexible configuration systems enables creation of scripts that can handle diverse target requirements, scanning preferences, and operational constraints through configuration files or command-line parameters.

External configuration files provide advantages for scripts that need to support multiple scanning profiles or that are used by multiple team members with different preferences. Configuration files enable customization of scanning parameters, target definitions, and output formats without requiring script modifications, making scripts more maintainable and user-friendly.

Error handling architecture design ensures that scripts can handle the various failure modes encountered during network scanning operations while maintaining appropriate logging and recovery capabilities. Network scanning operations encounter numerous potential failure points including network timeouts, target unreachability, and resource exhaustion that require comprehensive error handling to ensure reliable operation.

The implementation of robust error handling requires consideration of error detection, logging, recovery, and user notification across all script components. Effective error handling enables scripts to continue operating when encountering partial failures while providing clear feedback about problems that require attention or intervention.

Target Management and Input Processing

Effective target management enables scripts to handle diverse target specifications while implementing appropriate validation and preprocessing that ensures scanning operations proceed efficiently and safely. The ability to process targets from multiple sources and formats increases script flexibility while reducing the manual effort required for scan preparation.

Input validation and sanitization prevent scripts from attempting operations on invalid targets while protecting against input that might cause unexpected behavior or security issues. Understanding how to implement comprehensive input validation enables creation of scripts that behave predictably even when receiving malformed or potentially malicious input data.

Target format standardization enables scripts to process targets consistently regardless of their original specification format. Understanding how to normalize different target specification formats enables creation of scripts that can accept targets as individual addresses, network ranges, hostnames, or combinations of these formats while processing them through consistent internal logic.

Network range expansion converts CIDR notation and other range specifications into individual target addresses that can be processed systematically. Understanding how to implement efficient range expansion enables scripts to handle large target sets while managing memory usage and processing time appropriately.

Hostname resolution for target processing requires careful consideration of DNS timeouts, failure handling, and caching to ensure that scripts can process mixed hostname and IP address targets efficiently. Understanding how to implement robust hostname resolution enables scripts to handle targets specified in various formats while maintaining reasonable performance characteristics.

Target prioritization and ordering can improve scanning efficiency by processing targets in orders that optimize network usage, respect rate limiting requirements, or prioritize higher-value targets. Understanding how to implement intelligent target ordering enables creation of scripts that make efficient use of available time and resources while maximizing information gathering potential.

Duplicate target detection and elimination prevent scripts from wasting time scanning the same targets multiple times when target lists contain overlapping specifications. Understanding how to implement efficient duplicate detection enables processing of target lists from multiple sources while avoiding redundant scanning operations.

Scanning Implementation and Process Management

The core scanning functionality represents the heart of the port scanning script and requires careful implementation that balances scan thoroughness with performance, stealth, and reliability considerations. Understanding how to implement effective scanning logic enables creation of scripts that can adapt their approach based on target characteristics and scanning requirements.

Scan type selection logic enables scripts to choose appropriate scanning techniques based on target characteristics, available time, and stealth requirements. Different scan types provide different advantages in terms of speed, stealth, and information gathering, making intelligent scan selection crucial for effective automation.

TCP connect scanning provides reliable connectivity testing that works through most network security controls but generates easily detectable connection attempts. Understanding when to use TCP connect scanning enables creation of scripts that can gather reliable connectivity information while accepting the trade-offs in terms of stealth and detection risk.

SYN scanning offers improved stealth characteristics compared to full TCP connections while providing reliable port state information for most targets. Understanding how to implement SYN scanning effectively enables creation of scripts that balance stealth requirements with information gathering needs while handling the various responses that different targets might generate.

UDP scanning presents unique challenges in terms of response interpretation and timing due to the connectionless nature of UDP and the tendency of many systems to silently drop UDP packets rather than responding with explicit rejections. Understanding how to implement effective UDP scanning enables comprehensive port coverage while managing the timing and reliability challenges associated with UDP scanning.

Port range management enables scripts to focus scanning efforts on ports most likely to yield valuable information while providing options for comprehensive coverage when time and resources permit. Understanding how to implement flexible port range selection enables creation of scripts that can adapt their coverage based on scanning objectives and available resources.

Custom port lists provide advantages for focused scanning scenarios where specific services or vulnerabilities are of particular interest. Understanding how to implement custom port list support enables creation of scripts that can optimize their scanning approach based on engagement objectives or threat intelligence information.

Timing and rate limiting implementation ensures that scripts operate within acceptable network usage bounds while avoiding triggering security controls that might block scanning activities. Understanding how to implement effective timing controls enables creation of scripts that balance scanning speed with stealth and reliability requirements.

Logging and Result Management

Comprehensive logging capabilities enable scripts to maintain detailed records of scanning activities while providing multiple output formats that support different analysis and reporting requirements. Effective logging design ensures that important information is captured and preserved while maintaining reasonable storage requirements and enabling efficient analysis of results.

Multi-level logging enables scripts to capture different types of information at appropriate detail levels while providing flexibility in terms of what information is preserved and how it is organized. Understanding how to implement effective logging hierarchies enables creation of scripts that can provide detailed troubleshooting information when needed while maintaining concise operational logs for routine use.

Operational logging captures information about script execution including start times, target processing progress, scan completion status, and overall statistics that provide visibility into script operation and performance. This level of logging enables monitoring of script execution and identification of performance or reliability issues.

Result logging preserves detailed information about scan findings including discovered services, response times, and service characteristics that provide the primary output of scanning operations. Understanding how to structure result logging enables creation of scripts that produce useful output while maintaining appropriate detail levels.

Debug logging captures detailed information about script operation including decision logic, error conditions, and intermediate processing results that support troubleshooting and script optimization. Debug logging should be designed to be activated selectively to avoid overwhelming storage and processing resources during normal operation.

Output format flexibility enables scripts to produce results in multiple formats that support different analysis and integration requirements. Understanding how to implement multiple output formats enables creation of scripts that can integrate with various analysis tools and reporting systems while maintaining human-readable output for interactive use.

Structured output formats like JSON or XML enable integration with other tools and automated analysis systems while preserving all scan data in formats that can be processed programmatically. Understanding how to implement structured output enables creation of scripts that can serve as components in larger automation workflows.

Human-readable output formats provide summary information and highlights that enable rapid assessment of scan results without requiring detailed analysis of raw scan data. Understanding how to create effective summary reporting enables creation of scripts that provide actionable intelligence while maintaining access to detailed supporting data.

Writing Your Own Recon Toolkit

Developing a comprehensive reconnaissance toolkit represents the culmination of automation skills covered throughout this chapter and demonstrates how individual tools and techniques can be integrated into professional-quality automation frameworks. A well-designed reconnaissance toolkit provides consistent interfaces, coordinated execution, and integrated analysis capabilities that significantly improve efficiency and effectiveness compared to ad-hoc tool usage.

Framework Design and Architecture

Creating an effective reconnaissance framework requires careful consideration of how different reconnaissance activities relate to each other and how their results can be integrated to provide comprehensive intelligence about target environments. The framework architecture determines the toolkit's flexibility, maintainability, and ability to evolve as reconnaissance requirements and techniques change over time.

Workflow orchestration design enables the toolkit to coordinate different reconnaissance activities in logical sequences that build upon each other's results while managing dependencies and failure conditions appropriately. Understanding how to design effective workflow orchestration enables creation of toolkits that can adapt their approach based on initial findings while maintaining appropriate boundaries on scope and execution time.

The implementation of intelligent workflow orchestration requires understanding how different reconnaissance activities depend on each other and how their results can inform subsequent activities. Initial host discovery might determine the scope for port scanning, while DNS enumeration results could identify additional targets for network scanning activities.

Plugin architecture design enables the toolkit to support different reconnaissance techniques through standardized interfaces that allow new capabilities to be added without modifying core framework code. Understanding how to design effective plugin architectures enables creation of extensible frameworks that can evolve to incorporate new techniques and tools as they become available.

Plugin interfaces should provide standardized methods for configuration, execution, result reporting, and error handling that enable consistent integration of different reconnaissance techniques. Effective plugin interfaces balance standardization with flexibility, enabling diverse techniques to integrate cleanly while maintaining their unique capabilities and requirements.

Data management architecture design addresses how the toolkit stores, organizes, and provides access to reconnaissance results while supporting analysis activities and integration with external tools. Understanding how to design effective data management enables creation of toolkits that can handle large amounts of reconnaissance data while maintaining performance and enabling sophisticated analysis capabilities.

Result correlation capabilities enable the toolkit to identify relationships between findings from different reconnaissance activities, providing insights that might not be apparent when analyzing individual tool outputs separately. Understanding how to implement effective correlation enables creation of toolkits that provide intelligence rather than just raw reconnaissance data.

Integration of Multiple Reconnaissance Techniques

Effective reconnaissance toolkits integrate multiple information gathering techniques into coordinated workflows that leverage the strengths of different approaches while compensating for their individual limitations. Understanding how to combine different techniques effectively enables creation of comprehensive reconnaissance capabilities that provide thorough coverage of target environments.

Passive reconnaissance integration enables the toolkit to gather information through techniques that do not generate traffic directed at target systems, reducing detection risk while providing valuable intelligence about target infrastructure and operations. Understanding how to integrate passive techniques effectively enables creation of toolkits that can gather substantial intelligence while maintaining low profiles.

Open-source intelligence (OSINT) integration leverages publicly available information sources to gather intelligence about target organizations, their personnel, infrastructure, and operations. Understanding how to integrate OSINT techniques programmatically enables creation of toolkits that can automate information gathering from diverse public sources while correlating findings with technical reconnaissance results.

Search engine reconnaissance provides information about target web presence, exposed documents, and infrastructure details that might not be discoverable through direct technical scanning. Understanding how to automate search engine reconnaissance enables creation of toolkits that can systematically explore target web presence while respecting search engine terms of service and rate limiting requirements.

Social media and public records analysis can reveal information about target organizations, their personnel, and business relationships that provides context for technical reconnaissance findings. Understanding how to integrate social media analysis appropriately enables creation of comprehensive reconnaissance capabilities while respecting privacy and legal boundaries.

Active reconnaissance integration coordinates direct information gathering techniques that generate traffic directed at target systems, requiring careful consideration of detection risk, target impact, and legal considerations. Understanding how to integrate active techniques responsibly enables creation of toolkits that can gather detailed technical information while managing associated risks appropriately.

Network scanning integration combines different scanning techniques to provide comprehensive coverage of target network infrastructure while managing scan timing, target load, and detection risk. Understanding how to coordinate multiple scanning approaches enables creation of toolkits that maximize information gathering while operating within acceptable risk and impact boundaries.

Service enumeration integration builds upon network scanning results to gather detailed information about discovered services, their configurations, and potential vulnerabilities. Understanding how to integrate service enumeration effectively enables creation of toolkits that provide actionable intelligence about discovered systems and services.

Advanced Analysis and Correlation Capabilities

Beyond basic reconnaissance data collection, advanced toolkits implement analysis capabilities that identify patterns, correlate findings across different sources, and provide intelligence that supports decision-making throughout security assessment processes. Understanding how to implement effective analysis capabilities distinguishes professional-quality toolkits from simple tool aggregations.

Pattern recognition capabilities enable toolkits to identify naming conventions, network architecture patterns, and organizational structures that provide insights into target infrastructure and operations. Understanding how to implement pattern recognition enables creation of toolkits that can identify valuable intelligence that might not be apparent through manual analysis of large datasets.

Network topology analysis combines information from various reconnaissance activities to construct understanding of how target networks are organized and how different systems relate to each other. Understanding how to implement topology analysis enables creation of toolkits that provide strategic intelligence about target infrastructure rather than just tactical information about individual systems.

Infrastructure fingerprinting analysis identifies technologies, configurations, and architectural patterns that provide insights into target security posture and potential attack vectors. Understanding how to implement fingerprinting analysis enables creation of toolkits that can assess target environments systematically while identifying opportunities and risks.

Vulnerability correlation capabilities enable toolkits to combine service detection results with vulnerability databases to identify potential security issues that require attention. Understanding how to implement vulnerability correlation enables creation of toolkits that provide actionable security intelligence rather than just raw reconnaissance data.

Risk assessment integration enables toolkits to evaluate reconnaissance findings in the context of potential security risks and business impact, providing prioritized intelligence that supports decision-making about security assessment activities. Understanding how to implement risk assessment capabilities enables creation of toolkits that provide strategic value beyond basic information gathering.

Threat intelligence integration enables toolkits to correlate reconnaissance findings with known threat indicators, providing context about potential threats and attack techniques that might be relevant to target environments. Understanding how to integrate threat intelligence enables creation of toolkits that provide current, actionable intelligence about potential security threats.

Reporting and Output Generation

Professional reconnaissance toolkits implement comprehensive reporting capabilities that present findings in formats appropriate for different audiences and use cases. Understanding how to design effective reporting capabilities ensures that reconnaissance intelligence is communicated clearly and supports decision-making throughout security assessment processes.

Executive summary reporting provides high-level overviews of reconnaissance findings that focus on strategic implications and business risks rather than technical details. Understanding how to create effective executive summaries enables communication of reconnaissance intelligence to business stakeholders who need to understand security implications without requiring technical expertise.

Technical reporting provides detailed information about reconnaissance findings including specific systems, services, configurations, and potential vulnerabilities that support technical analysis and security assessment activities. Understanding how to create comprehensive technical reports enables communication of detailed intelligence to technical audiences who need complete information for their activities.

Visual representation capabilities enable presentation of reconnaissance findings through charts, graphs, network diagrams, and other visual formats that communicate complex information effectively. Understanding how to implement effective visualization enables creation of reports that communicate reconnaissance intelligence clearly while supporting rapid understanding of target environments.

Network topology visualization provides graphical representations of discovered network infrastructure that enable rapid understanding of target network organization and system relationships. Understanding how to create effective network visualizations enables communication of infrastructure intelligence through formats that support strategic planning and tactical execution.

Timeline analysis visualization presents reconnaissance findings in temporal context that enables understanding of how target infrastructure has evolved over time and identification of patterns that might indicate operational cycles or security changes. Understanding how to implement timeline analysis enables creation of intelligence products that provide historical context for current findings.

Export format flexibility enables reconnaissance toolkits to produce results in multiple formats that support integration with other tools and analysis systems. Understanding how to implement multiple export formats enables creation of toolkits that can integrate effectively with existing security infrastructure while maintaining standalone utility.

API integration capabilities enable reconnaissance toolkits to share results with other security tools and systems programmatically, supporting automation workflows that incorporate reconnaissance activities as components of larger security operations. Understanding how to implement API integration enables creation of toolkits that serve as components in comprehensive security automation frameworks.

Conclusion

This chapter has established a comprehensive foundation for automating reconnaissance and scanning activities that forms the cornerstone of effective cybersecurity automation. From mastering Nmap automation and DNS intelligence gathering to building complete reconnaissance frameworks, you've developed skills that will serve as building blocks for increasingly sophisticated security automation projects throughout your career.

The progression from individual tool automation to integrated reconnaissance frameworks demonstrates how fundamental scripting capabilities can be combined to create professional-quality automation solutions. The techniques covered in this chapter—automated scanning, intelligent result parsing, multi-source intelligence correlation, and comprehensive reporting—represent core competencies that distinguish effective security professionals from those who rely solely on manual processes.

The reconnaissance toolkit developed in the final section provides a practical template for creating comprehensive automation frameworks that can adapt to various engagement requirements while maintaining professional standards for logging, error handling, and result presentation. This toolkit demonstrates how the individual techniques covered throughout the chapter combine to create capabilities that significantly exceed the sum of their parts.

The automation skills developed in this chapter enable efficient handling of reconnaissance tasks that would otherwise consume substantial time and effort while providing more comprehensive and consistent results than manual approaches. More importantly, these automation capabilities free security professionals to focus on analysis, decision-making, and strategic activities that require human expertise while delegating routine information gathering to reliable automated systems.

Moving forward, the reconnaissance automation capabilities established in this chapter provide the foundation for more advanced automation projects including vulnerability assessment workflows, incident response tools, and security monitoring systems. The patterns and practices demonstrated here—modular design, comprehensive error handling, flexible configuration management, and professional reporting—will serve as templates for all future automation development while ensuring that your tools maintain the reliability and professionalism required for cybersecurity operations.

The investment you've made in understanding these reconnaissance automation techniques will pay dividends throughout your cybersecurity career as you encounter new challenges that can be addressed through systematic information gathering and analysis. With these capabilities firmly established, you're ready to explore more advanced automation topics that build upon this reconnaissance foundation while addressing other critical areas of cybersecurity operations.

Chapter 3: Scripting for Hardening and Compliance

System hardening and compliance management represent critical aspects of cybersecurity that require consistent, systematic approaches to maintain secure configurations across diverse computing environments. The challenge of maintaining security baselines, implementing compliance requirements, and monitoring for configuration drift becomes exponentially more complex as organizations scale their infrastructure and face increasingly sophisticated threats. Manual approaches to hardening and compliance management simply cannot keep pace with the rate of change in modern IT environments or provide the consistency and reliability required for effective security operations.

Bash scripting provides powerful capabilities for automating hardening processes, implementing compliance checks, and maintaining security configurations at scale. Unlike GUI-based management tools that often impose rigid workflows and limited customization options, shell scripts can be tailored precisely to organizational requirements while integrating seamlessly with existing infrastructure and processes. The ability to automate routine hardening tasks, systematically verify compliance status, and respond quickly to security configuration issues enables security teams to focus their expertise on strategic initiatives rather than repetitive maintenance activities.

This chapter explores comprehensive approaches to automating system hardening and compliance management through sophisticated Bash scripting techniques. Rather than covering basic security configurations that are well-documented elsewhere, we focus on creating intelligent automation that can adapt to different system types, handle varying compliance requirements, and provide detailed reporting that supports audit and risk management activities. The scripts and frameworks developed throughout this chapter demonstrate professional-level automation capabilities while addressing real-world challenges encountered in enterprise security operations.

The progression through this chapter builds from foundational automation concepts like patch management and configuration scanning to advanced topics including comprehensive hardening frameworks and intelligent monitoring systems. Each section introduces new automation techniques while reinforcing fundamental principles, ensuring that your scripting capabilities develop systematically while maintaining focus on practical security applications that provide immediate value to cybersecurity operations.

Auto-Patching and Updating Linux Systems

Patch management represents one of the most critical aspects of system security, yet it remains one of the most challenging to implement effectively at scale. The complexity of managing patches across diverse Linux distributions, handling dependency conflicts, managing downtime requirements, and ensuring patch compatibility creates significant operational challenges that demand automated solutions. Effective patch management automation must balance security requirements with operational stability while providing comprehensive reporting and rollback capabilities for situations where patches cause unexpected issues.

Understanding Patch Management Fundamentals

Effective patch management automation requires thorough understanding of how different Linux distributions handle package management, how security updates are prioritized and distributed, and how automated patching systems can be designed to minimize risk while maintaining security currency. The diversity of package management systems across different Linux distributions creates complexity that automation scripts must handle gracefully while maintaining consistent security outcomes.

Package management system integration forms the foundation of effective patch automation because different distributions use different tools, repositories, and update mechanisms. Understanding how to create automation scripts that can work effectively across multiple package management systems enables deployment of consistent patch management processes regardless of the underlying distribution. This cross-platform capability becomes particularly important in heterogeneous environments where multiple Linux distributions are deployed for different purposes.

The APT package management system used by Debian and Ubuntu distributions provides sophisticated dependency resolution and package state management that enables reliable automated patching when properly integrated with monitoring and verification systems. Understanding how to leverage APT's capabilities effectively enables creation of robust patch management workflows that can handle complex dependency relationships while maintaining system stability.

YUM and DNF package managers used by Red Hat Enterprise Linux, CentOS, and Fedora distributions offer different capabilities and command structures that require specific integration approaches for effective automation. Understanding how to work with these package managers enables creation of patch management systems that can operate effectively across Red Hat-based environments while leveraging distribution-specific features.

Package repository management becomes crucial for enterprise patch management because organizations often need to control patch deployment timing, test patches in staging environments, and maintain consistent package versions across different system types. Understanding how to integrate repository management into patch automation enables creation of comprehensive patch management workflows that support organizational change management processes.

Security update prioritization requires understanding how different distributions classify and distribute security patches, enabling automation scripts to distinguish between critical security updates that require immediate deployment and routine updates that can be scheduled during maintenance windows. This prioritization capability enables creation of patch management systems that can respond appropriately to different types of security threats while maintaining operational stability.

Automated Update Strategies and Implementation

Implementing effective automated update strategies requires careful consideration of organizational requirements, system criticality, and operational constraints while maintaining appropriate safeguards against patch-related disruptions. The design of automated update systems must balance security currency with operational stability while providing comprehensive monitoring and rollback capabilities.

Staged rollout strategies enable deployment of patches to representative test systems before broader deployment, providing opportunities to identify compatibility issues and verify patch effectiveness before impacting production systems. Understanding how to implement intelligent staged rollout enables creation of patch management systems that minimize deployment risk while maintaining reasonable deployment timelines for critical security updates.

The implementation of effective staged rollouts requires understanding how to classify systems appropriately, define representative test environments, and establish criteria for promoting patches from testing to production deployment. This systematic approach enables identification of potential issues before they impact critical systems while ensuring that security updates are deployed within appropriate timeframes.

Maintenance window management enables scheduling of patch deployment activities during predetermined periods when system downtime or performance impact can be accommodated within operational requirements. Understanding how to integrate maintenance window management into patch automation enables creation of systems that respect organizational operational constraints while ensuring that security updates are deployed consistently.

Automated rollback capabilities provide essential safety mechanisms for situations where patches cause unexpected issues or compatibility problems. Understanding how to implement reliable rollback mechanisms enables creation of patch management systems that can recover quickly from patch-related problems while minimizing operational impact.

The implementation of automated rollback requires understanding how different package management systems handle package state management and how to preserve system states that enable reliable recovery from problematic patches. This capability becomes particularly important for critical systems where patch-related disruptions must be minimized while maintaining security currency.

Emergency patching procedures enable rapid deployment of critical security updates outside normal maintenance windows when security threats require immediate response. Understanding how to implement emergency patching capabilities enables creation of patch management systems that can respond appropriately to critical security vulnerabilities while maintaining appropriate approval and verification processes.

Patch Testing and Validation Automation

Comprehensive patch testing and validation processes ensure that automated patch deployment maintains system functionality while implementing necessary security improvements. The complexity of modern software environments makes manual testing impractical for routine patch deployment, necessitating automated approaches that can verify system functionality efficiently while identifying potential issues before they impact operations.

Functional testing automation verifies that critical system functions continue to operate correctly after patch deployment, providing confidence that patches have not introduced unexpected compatibility issues or functionality problems. Understanding how to implement comprehensive functional testing enables creation of patch management systems that maintain high reliability while deploying security updates consistently.

The design of effective functional testing requires understanding how to identify critical system functions, create automated tests that verify functionality reliably, and establish criteria for determining when patch deployment should proceed or be rolled back based on test results. This systematic approach enables early identification of patch-related issues while maintaining deployment efficiency.

Service availability testing ensures that critical services remain accessible and responsive after patch deployment, providing verification that patches have not introduced performance issues or service disruptions. Understanding how to implement automated service testing enables creation of patch management systems that maintain service quality while implementing necessary security updates.

Configuration validation testing verifies that system configurations remain consistent with security baselines after patch deployment, ensuring that patches have not modified security settings or introduced configuration drift. Understanding how to implement configuration validation enables creation of patch management systems that maintain security posture while deploying updates systematically.

Performance impact assessment enables identification of patches that might affect system performance characteristics, providing information necessary to make informed decisions about patch deployment timing and potential mitigation measures. Understanding how to implement performance monitoring enables creation of patch management systems that maintain operational performance while implementing security improvements.

Security validation testing verifies that deployed patches provide expected security improvements and have not introduced new vulnerabilities or security configuration issues. Understanding how to implement security validation enables creation of patch management systems that achieve their primary security objectives while maintaining overall system security posture.

Enterprise-Scale Patch Management Orchestration

Large-scale patch management requires sophisticated orchestration capabilities that can coordinate patch deployment across hundreds or thousands of systems while managing dependencies, maintaining operational requirements, and providing comprehensive reporting for audit and compliance purposes. Understanding how to implement enterprise-scale orchestration enables creation of patch management systems that can handle organizational complexity while maintaining security effectiveness.

Parallel deployment management enables efficient patch deployment across large numbers of systems while respecting infrastructure capacity limits and avoiding overwhelming network or repository resources. Understanding how to implement intelligent parallel deployment enables creation of patch management systems that optimize deployment efficiency while maintaining system stability.

The implementation of effective parallel deployment requires understanding how to classify systems appropriately, manage deployment queues intelligently, and coordinate resource usage across multiple deployment streams. This systematic approach enables efficient patch deployment while avoiding resource contention and deployment bottlenecks.

Dependency management enables coordination of patch deployment across systems with interdependencies, ensuring that patches are deployed in appropriate sequences that maintain system functionality and avoid dependency conflicts. Understanding how to implement dependency management enables creation of patch management systems that handle complex infrastructure relationships effectively.

Progress monitoring and reporting capabilities provide visibility into patch deployment status across large numbers of systems, enabling operational teams to track deployment progress and identify systems that require attention or intervention. Understanding how to implement comprehensive monitoring enables creation of patch management systems that provide appropriate operational visibility while maintaining deployment efficiency.

Failure handling and recovery mechanisms enable automated responses to patch deployment failures while providing escalation paths for situations that require human intervention. Understanding how to implement robust failure handling enables creation of patch management systems that maintain high reliability while minimizing operational overhead for routine deployment activities.

Compliance reporting integration ensures that patch management activities are documented appropriately for audit and regulatory compliance purposes while providing management visibility into security posture and patch currency across the organization. Understanding how to implement compliance reporting enables creation of patch management systems that support organizational governance requirements while maintaining operational efficiency.

Scanning for Misconfigurations and Insecure Permissions

Configuration assessment and permission auditing represent fundamental security activities that require systematic approaches to identify potential vulnerabilities and ensure compliance with security baselines. The complexity of modern Linux systems, with their numerous configuration files, service settings, and permission structures, makes manual assessment impractical for comprehensive security evaluation. Automated scanning approaches enable consistent, thorough assessment while providing detailed documentation of findings that support remediation and compliance activities.

File System Permission Analysis

File system permissions form a critical component of Linux security, controlling access to files, directories, and system resources in ways that can significantly impact overall system security posture. Understanding how to automate comprehensive permission analysis enables identification of potential security issues while providing detailed documentation that supports remediation planning and compliance verification.

Permission scanning strategies must account for the diverse ways that inappropriate permissions can create security vulnerabilities, from world-writable files that enable unauthorized modification to overly restrictive permissions that interfere with legitimate system operation. Understanding how to implement comprehensive permission scanning enables identification of permission-related security issues while minimizing false positives that reduce scanner effectiveness.

Systematic file system traversal requires careful consideration of performance, resource usage, and scope management to ensure that permission scanning operations complete efficiently while covering all relevant system areas. Understanding how to implement efficient traversal strategies enables creation of scanning systems that can handle large file systems while maintaining reasonable execution times and resource usage.

The implementation of effective file system traversal requires understanding how to optimize directory traversal algorithms, manage memory usage during large-scale scanning operations, and handle special file types and mount points appropriately. This systematic approach enables comprehensive coverage while maintaining scanning efficiency and reliability.

World-writable file detection identifies files and directories that allow write access to all users, creating potential security vulnerabilities where unauthorized users might modify critical files or inject malicious content. Understanding how to implement world-writable file detection enables identification of significant security risks while providing detailed information necessary for remediation planning.

Setuid and setgid binary identification locates executable files with special permission bits that enable privilege escalation, requiring careful assessment to ensure that these permissions are appropriate and necessary for system operation. Understanding how to implement setuid scanning enables identification of potential privilege escalation vectors while providing information necessary for security assessment and hardening activities.

Permission anomaly detection identifies files and directories with unusual permission patterns that might indicate security issues, configuration errors, or unauthorized modifications. Understanding how to implement anomaly detection enables identification of subtle permission issues that might not be caught by standard permission checks while providing comprehensive security assessment capabilities.

Configuration File Security Assessment

Configuration files contain critical security settings that control system behavior, service operation, and access controls in ways that significantly impact overall security posture. Automated configuration assessment enables systematic evaluation of security settings while providing detailed documentation that supports compliance verification and security improvement activities.

Critical configuration file identification enables focused assessment of files that have the greatest impact on system security, ensuring that scanning resources are allocated effectively while maintaining comprehensive coverage of important security settings. Understanding how to implement intelligent configuration file identification enables creation of scanning systems that provide thorough security assessment while maintaining efficiency and focus.

The identification of critical configuration files requires understanding how different services and system components store their configuration data and which settings have the greatest security implications. This knowledge enables creation of scanning systems that focus attention on configurations most likely to impact security posture while providing comprehensive coverage of important system areas.

Security setting validation enables verification that configuration files contain appropriate security settings and do not include configurations that might create vulnerabilities or compliance issues. Understanding how to implement security setting validation enables creation of scanning systems that provide actionable security intelligence while supporting compliance verification activities.

Configuration file permission assessment ensures that configuration files themselves are protected appropriately and cannot be modified by unauthorized users or processes. Understanding how to implement configuration file permission assessment enables identification of vulnerabilities where attackers might modify configuration files to compromise system security.

Default credential detection identifies configuration files that contain default passwords, authentication tokens, or other credentials that create significant security vulnerabilities. Understanding how to implement credential detection enables identification of critical security issues while providing detailed information necessary for immediate remediation.

Encryption and authentication configuration assessment verifies that systems are configured to use appropriate encryption protocols, authentication mechanisms, and security controls that protect against common attack vectors. Understanding how to implement encryption configuration assessment enables verification of critical security controls while identifying areas where security improvements are needed.

Service and Daemon Security Analysis

Running services and daemons represent significant components of system attack surface, making their security configuration critical for overall system security posture. Automated service analysis enables comprehensive assessment of service configurations while identifying potential vulnerabilities and compliance issues that require attention.

Service enumeration and classification enables systematic assessment of all running services while focusing analysis efforts on services that present the greatest security risks or compliance requirements. Understanding how to implement comprehensive service analysis enables creation of scanning systems that provide thorough security assessment while maintaining efficiency and relevance.

The implementation of effective service enumeration requires understanding how different Linux distributions manage services and how to identify service characteristics that impact security assessment priorities. This systematic approach enables focused analysis while maintaining comprehensive coverage of important security considerations.

Network service exposure analysis identifies services that are accessible over network connections, enabling assessment of external attack surface and verification that only necessary services are exposed to network access. Understanding how to implement network service analysis enables identification of potential attack vectors while providing information necessary for network security planning.

Service configuration security assessment verifies that individual services are configured securely and do not include settings that might create vulnerabilities or compliance issues. Understanding how to implement service configuration assessment enables identification of service-specific security issues while providing detailed information necessary for remediation planning.

Authentication and authorization configuration analysis ensures that services implement appropriate access controls and do not allow unauthorized access or privilege escalation. Understanding how to implement authentication analysis enables verification of critical security controls while identifying areas where access controls might be strengthened.

Service version and vulnerability assessment correlates running service versions with known vulnerability databases to identify services that might be vulnerable to known security issues. Understanding how to implement vulnerability correlation enables identification of immediate security risks while providing prioritized information for patch management and security improvement activities.

System-Wide Security Configuration Auditing

Comprehensive security auditing requires systematic assessment of system-wide security configurations that affect overall security posture beyond individual files or services. Understanding how to implement system-wide auditing enables identification of security issues that might not be apparent through component-specific assessments while providing holistic security evaluation capabilities.

Kernel security parameter assessment verifies that kernel security features are enabled appropriately and configured to provide effective protection against common attack techniques. Understanding how to implement kernel parameter assessment enables verification of fundamental security controls while identifying opportunities for security improvements.

System hardening verification ensures that standard security hardening measures have been implemented consistently and are functioning correctly across different system components. Understanding how to implement hardening verification enables systematic assessment of security posture while providing detailed documentation for compliance and audit purposes.

Network security configuration analysis evaluates system-wide network security settings including firewall configurations, network service restrictions, and communication security controls. Understanding how to implement network security analysis enables assessment of network-related security controls while identifying potential improvements to network security posture.

Access control mechanism verification ensures that system access controls are configured appropriately and functioning effectively to prevent unauthorized access and privilege escalation. Understanding how to implement access control verification enables assessment of fundamental security mechanisms while identifying areas where access controls might be strengthened.

Logging and monitoring configuration assessment verifies that security logging is enabled appropriately and configured to capture security-relevant events effectively. Understanding how to implement logging assessment enables verification of security monitoring capabilities while identifying gaps in security event detection and documentation.

Writing a Basic System Hardening Checklist in Bash

Creating a comprehensive system hardening checklist implemented through Bash scripting provides a systematic approach to implementing security improvements while ensuring consistency and repeatability across multiple systems. A well-designed hardening script serves as both an implementation tool and documentation system, providing clear records of security improvements while enabling efficient deployment of security configurations across diverse environments.

Hardening Framework Design and Architecture

Effective hardening frameworks require careful architectural design that balances comprehensiveness with flexibility while providing appropriate safeguards against unintended system modifications. The framework architecture determines the script's ability to handle different system types, adapt to varying requirements, and provide reliable results across diverse deployment scenarios.

Modular hardening approach enables creation of hardening frameworks that can address different security domains independently while providing coordinated implementation of comprehensive security improvements. Understanding how to implement modular hardening enables creation of frameworks that can be customized for different environments while maintaining systematic approaches to security improvement.

The implementation of modular hardening requires understanding how different security controls interact with each other and how to sequence hardening activities to avoid conflicts or dependencies that might interfere with successful implementation. This systematic approach enables reliable hardening while maintaining flexibility for different deployment scenarios.

Configuration backup and restore capabilities ensure that hardening activities can be reversed if they cause unexpected issues or if system requirements change after hardening implementation. Understanding how to implement reliable backup and restore capabilities enables creation of hardening frameworks that minimize implementation risk while providing recovery options for problematic configurations.

Hardening verification and validation ensure that implemented security improvements are functioning correctly and providing expected security benefits. Understanding how to implement comprehensive verification enables creation of hardening frameworks that provide confidence in security improvements while identifying areas where additional attention might be required.

Risk assessment and prioritization enables hardening frameworks to focus their efforts on security improvements that provide the greatest security benefits while managing implementation complexity and potential operational impact. Understanding how to implement risk-based prioritization enables creation of hardening frameworks that maximize security improvement effectiveness while minimizing implementation overhead.

Compliance mapping capabilities enable hardening frameworks to document how their security improvements support specific compliance requirements, providing audit trail information and ensuring that hardening activities address relevant regulatory and organizational standards. Understanding how to implement compliance mapping enables creation of hardening frameworks that support governance requirements while providing security improvements.

Core Security Hardening Components

Comprehensive system hardening requires systematic implementation of security improvements across multiple system areas, from basic file permissions and service configurations to advanced security features and monitoring capabilities. Understanding how to implement core hardening components enables creation of frameworks that provide fundamental security improvements while establishing foundations for more advanced security measures.

User account and authentication hardening strengthens user management and authentication mechanisms to prevent unauthorized access and reduce the impact of compromised credentials. Understanding how to implement authentication hardening enables creation of frameworks that establish strong access controls while maintaining usability for legitimate users.

Password policy implementation ensures that user accounts use strong passwords and follow organizational password requirements while providing mechanisms for password management and enforcement. Understanding how to implement password policies enables creation of hardening frameworks that strengthen authentication security while supporting user productivity and compliance requirements.

Account lockout and monitoring implementation provides protection against brute force attacks while enabling detection of unauthorized access attempts. Understanding how to implement account security monitoring enables creation of hardening frameworks that provide both preventive and detective security controls for user account protection.

Network service hardening reduces system attack surface by disabling unnecessary services and configuring required services securely. Understanding how to implement service hardening enables creation of frameworks that minimize network exposure while maintaining necessary system functionality.

Service configuration security improvement ensures that required network services are configured with appropriate security settings and do not expose unnecessary functionality or information. Understanding how to implement service security configuration enables creation of hardening frameworks that maintain necessary functionality while minimizing security risks.

Firewall configuration implementation provides network-level access controls that restrict network communication to necessary protocols and destinations. Understanding how to implement firewall hardening enables creation of frameworks that provide network security controls while maintaining necessary connectivity for system operation.

File system and permission hardening strengthens file system security through appropriate permission settings, access controls, and monitoring capabilities. Understanding how to implement file system hardening enables creation of frameworks that protect critical system files while maintaining necessary access for system operation and administration.

Advanced Hardening Implementation Techniques

Beyond basic security improvements, advanced hardening techniques implement sophisticated security controls that provide defense-in-depth protection against advanced threats while maintaining system functionality and performance. Understanding how to implement advanced hardening techniques enables creation of comprehensive security frameworks that provide enterprise-level protection.

Kernel security enhancement implementation enables advanced security features that provide protection against kernel-level attacks and privilege escalation attempts. Understanding how to implement kernel hardening enables creation of frameworks that provide fundamental security improvements while maintaining system stability and performance.

Security module configuration enables implementation of advanced access control systems like SELinux or AppArmor that provide fine-grained control over system resource access. Understanding how to implement security module configuration enables creation of hardening frameworks that provide sophisticated access controls while maintaining system usability.

Intrusion detection and prevention system integration enables real-time monitoring and response capabilities that can detect and respond to security threats automatically. Understanding how to implement intrusion detection integration enables creation of hardening frameworks that provide both preventive and responsive security capabilities.

Cryptographic configuration hardening ensures that system cryptographic capabilities are configured securely and use appropriate algorithms and key management practices. Understanding how to implement cryptographic hardening enables creation of frameworks that provide strong data protection while maintaining system performance and interoperability.

System monitoring and alerting implementation provides visibility into system security status and enables rapid response to security events or configuration changes. Understanding how to implement security monitoring enables creation of hardening frameworks that provide ongoing security oversight while supporting incident response capabilities.

Compliance and audit trail implementation ensures that hardening activities are documented appropriately, and that ongoing system operation maintains compliance with relevant security standards. Understanding how to implement compliance monitoring enables creation of hardening frameworks that support governance requirements while providing security improvements.

Testing and Validation Procedures

Comprehensive testing and validation procedures ensure that hardening implementations provide expected security benefits while maintaining system functionality and performance. Understanding how to implement thorough testing enables creation of hardening frameworks that provide reliable security improvements while minimizing implementation risks.

Functional testing verification ensures that hardened systems continue to provide necessary functionality while implementing security improvements. Understanding how to implement comprehensive functional testing enables creation of hardening frameworks that maintain operational requirements while providing security benefits.

Security improvement validation verifies that implemented hardening measures are functioning correctly and providing expected security benefits. Understanding how to implement security validation enables creation of hardening frameworks that provide confidence in security improvements while identifying areas where additional attention might be required.

Performance impact assessment evaluates how hardening implementations affect system performance and resource usage, providing information necessary to optimize hardening configurations for different deployment scenarios. Understanding how to implement performance assessment enables creation of hardening frameworks that balance security improvements with operational requirements.

Rollback testing verification ensures that hardening frameworks can reliably reverse their implementations when necessary, providing confidence that hardening activities do not create irreversible system modifications. Understanding how to implement rollback testing enables creation of hardening frameworks that minimize implementation risk while providing recovery options for problematic configurations.

Creating Alert Scripts for Suspicious System Changes

Intelligent monitoring and alerting systems provide essential capabilities for detecting unauthorized changes, identifying potential security threats, and maintaining visibility into system security status over time. Effective alerting requires understanding how to distinguish between legitimate administrative activities and potentially malicious changes while providing timely notification of security-relevant events.

Change Detection and Monitoring Fundamentals

Effective change detection requires systematic monitoring of system components that are most likely to be modified during security incidents while avoiding excessive false positives that reduce alerting effectiveness. Understanding how to implement intelligent change detection enables creation of monitoring systems that provide valuable security intelligence while maintaining operational efficiency.

File integrity monitoring provides detection capabilities for unauthorized modifications to critical system files, configuration files, and executable programs. Understanding how to implement comprehensive file integrity monitoring enables detection of many common attack techniques while providing detailed information about the nature and scope of detected changes.

The implementation of effective file integrity monitoring requires understanding which files are most critical for security monitoring, how to establish reliable baselines for comparison, and how to distinguish between legitimate administrative changes and potentially malicious modifications. This systematic approach enables effective threat detection while minimizing false positive alerts that reduce monitoring effectiveness.

Configuration change detection monitors modifications to system configurations that might indicate unauthorized access or system compromise. Understanding how to implement configuration monitoring enables detection of changes that might not be apparent through other monitoring approaches while providing early warning of potential security issues.

Process and service monitoring provides detection capabilities for unauthorized processes, service modifications, and system behavior changes that might indicate malicious activity. Understanding how to implement process monitoring enables detection of many attack techniques while providing information about ongoing system activities that require investigation.

Network connection monitoring enables detection of unauthorized network communications, suspicious connection patterns, and potential data exfiltration activities. Understanding how to implement network monitoring enables detection of network-based attack activities while providing information about communication patterns that require security analysis.

User activity monitoring provides detection capabilities for unauthorized user activities, privilege escalation attempts, and suspicious authentication patterns. Understanding how to implement user activity monitoring enables detection of insider threats and compromised account activities while providing information about user behavior patterns that require security attention.

Real-Time Alerting Implementation

Real-time alerting capabilities ensure that security teams receive timely notification of potential threats while providing appropriate context and prioritization information that supports effective incident response. Understanding how to implement effective real-time alerting enables creation of monitoring systems that provide actionable security intelligence while avoiding alert fatigue.

Alert prioritization and classification enable monitoring systems to distinguish between different types of security events and provide appropriate urgency levels for different types of potential threats. Understanding how to implement intelligent prioritization enables creation of alerting systems that focus attention on the most critical security events while providing comprehensive coverage of potential threats.

The implementation of effective alert prioritization requires understanding how different types of system changes relate to various threat scenarios and how to assign appropriate risk levels based on the potential impact of detected changes. This systematic approach enables efficient allocation of security resources while ensuring that critical threats receive immediate attention.

Multi-channel notification capabilities ensure that critical security alerts reach appropriate personnel through reliable communication mechanisms while providing escalation paths for situations that require immediate attention. Understanding how to implement multi-channel alerting enables creation of monitoring systems that provide reliable notification while accommodating different communication preferences and availability patterns.

Alert correlation and aggregation capabilities prevent alert flooding by combining related alerts into comprehensive notifications while providing detailed information about the scope and nature of detected activities. Understanding how to implement alert correlation enables creation of monitoring systems that provide clear, actionable intelligence while avoiding information overload.

Context enrichment capabilities provide additional information about detected changes that supports rapid assessment and response decisions. Understanding how to implement context enrichment enables creation of alerting systems that provide comprehensive information necessary for effective incident response while maintaining notification efficiency.

Advanced Threat Detection Techniques

Advanced threat detection techniques enable identification of sophisticated attack activities that might not be detected through basic change monitoring approaches. Understanding how to implement advanced detection techniques enables creation of monitoring systems that provide comprehensive threat detection capabilities while maintaining appropriate performance and resource usage characteristics.

Behavioral analysis capabilities enable detection of suspicious activities based on deviations from normal system behavior patterns rather than specific signatures or rules. Understanding how to implement behavioral analysis enables detection of novel attack techniques while providing comprehensive coverage of potential threat activities.

The implementation of effective behavioral analysis requires understanding how to establish reliable baselines of normal system behavior and how to identify deviations that might indicate malicious activity while minimizing false positives from legitimate but unusual administrative activities. This approach enables detection of sophisticated threats while maintaining monitoring effectiveness.

Pattern recognition and correlation capabilities enable identification of attack patterns that span multiple system events or extend over longer time periods. Understanding how to implement pattern recognition enables detection of sophisticated attack campaigns while providing comprehensive threat intelligence that supports incident response and threat hunting activities.

Threat intelligence integration enables monitoring systems to correlate detected activities with known threat indicators and attack techniques, providing context that supports rapid threat assessment and response planning. Understanding how to implement threat intelligence integration enables creation of monitoring systems that provide current, actionable threat information while supporting strategic security planning.

Machine learning and statistical analysis capabilities enable detection of subtle patterns and anomalies that might not be apparent through rule-based detection approaches. Understanding how to implement machine learning techniques enables creation of monitoring systems that can adapt to evolving threat landscapes while providing sophisticated threat detection capabilities.

Incident Response Integration

Effective monitoring systems integrate seamlessly with incident response processes to ensure that detected threats are addressed systematically and effectively. Understanding how to implement incident response integration enables creation of monitoring systems that provide not just detection capabilities but also support coordinated response activities.

Automated response capabilities enable monitoring systems to implement immediate containment measures for certain types of detected threats while providing escalation paths for situations that require human intervention. Understanding how to implement automated response enables creation of monitoring systems that can respond rapidly to time-sensitive threats while maintaining appropriate oversight and control.

Evidence collection and preservation capabilities ensure that monitoring systems capture and preserve information necessary for incident investigation and forensic analysis. Understanding how to implement evidence collection enables creation of monitoring systems that support comprehensive incident response while maintaining legal and procedural requirements for evidence handling.

Communication and coordination capabilities enable monitoring systems to integrate with broader incident response workflows while providing appropriate notification and escalation mechanisms. Understanding how to implement response coordination enables creation of monitoring systems that support organizational incident response processes while providing effective threat detection and initial response capabilities.

Conclusion

This chapter has established comprehensive automation capabilities for system hardening and compliance management that enable systematic implementation of security improvements while maintaining operational efficiency and providing ongoing security monitoring. From automated patch management and configuration scanning to comprehensive hardening frameworks and intelligent change detection, you've developed skills that address critical aspects of cybersecurity operations while demonstrating advanced automation techniques.

The progression from individual security tasks to integrated hardening and monitoring frameworks demonstrates how fundamental scripting capabilities can be combined to create sophisticated security automation solutions. The techniques covered in this chapter—automated patch deployment, systematic security assessment, comprehensive hardening implementation, and intelligent threat detection—represent core competencies that enable effective security operations at enterprise scale.

The hardening framework and monitoring systems developed throughout this chapter provide practical templates for creating comprehensive security automation that can adapt to various organizational requirements while maintaining professional standards for reliability, reporting, and integration with existing security infrastructure. These frameworks demonstrate how individual automation techniques combine to create security capabilities that significantly exceed manual approaches in terms of consistency, coverage, and efficiency.

The automation skills developed in this chapter enable systematic implementation of security improvements and ongoing security monitoring that would otherwise require substantial manual effort while providing more comprehensive and consistent results than traditional approaches. More importantly, these automation capabilities enable security teams to focus their expertise on strategic security initiatives and threat response activities while delegating routine security maintenance to reliable automated systems.

Moving forward, the hardening and compliance automation capabilities established in this chapter provide the foundation for more advanced security automation projects including incident response workflows, threat hunting systems, and integrated security operations platforms. The patterns and practices demonstrated here—systematic assessment, risk-based prioritization, comprehensive documentation, and intelligent monitoring—will serve as templates for all future security automation development while ensuring that your tools maintain the reliability and effectiveness required for cybersecurity operations.

The investment you've made in understanding these hardening and compliance automation techniques will pay dividends throughout your cybersecurity career as you encounter new challenges that require systematic security improvement and ongoing monitoring capabilities. With these capabilities firmly established, you're ready to explore more advanced automation topics that build upon this security foundation while addressing other critical areas of cybersecurity operations such as incident response, threat analysis, and security operations center automation.

Chapter 4: Log Analysis and Incident Detection with Bash

Log analysis represents the cornerstone of effective cybersecurity monitoring and incident detection, providing the primary source of intelligence about system activities, security events, and potential threats. Modern computing environments generate enormous volumes of log data from diverse sources including operating systems, applications, network devices, and security tools, creating both opportunities and challenges for security professionals who must extract meaningful intelligence from this information deluge. The ability to process, analyze, and correlate log data efficiently determines the success of security monitoring programs and the speed at which threats can be detected and responded to effectively.

Traditional approaches to log analysis often rely on expensive commercial tools that, while powerful, may not provide the flexibility and customization capabilities required for unique organizational requirements or specialized security use cases. Bash scripting provides an alternative approach that leverages the powerful text processing capabilities inherent in Unix-like systems while enabling complete customization of analysis workflows. The combination of command-line tools like grep, awk, and sed with intelligent scripting creates sophisticated analysis capabilities that can be tailored precisely to specific security requirements while maintaining cost-effectiveness and operational flexibility.

This chapter explores comprehensive approaches to automating log analysis and incident detection through advanced Bash scripting techniques that demonstrate professional-level capabilities for processing large volumes of security data. Rather than covering basic text processing commands in isolation, we focus on creating intelligent analysis workflows that can identify patterns, correlate events across multiple sources, and provide actionable intelligence that supports rapid threat detection and incident response activities.

The progression through this chapter builds from fundamental text processing automation to sophisticated incident detection systems that integrate multiple analysis techniques while providing real-time monitoring capabilities. Each section introduces new analysis techniques while reinforcing scripting principles, ensuring that your log analysis capabilities develop systematically while maintaining focus on practical security applications that provide immediate value for cybersecurity operations.

Automating Grep, Awk, and Sed for Log Review

Text processing automation forms the foundation of effective log analysis, enabling systematic extraction of relevant information from large volumes of log data while filtering out noise and focusing attention on security-relevant events. The combination of grep, awk, and sed provides powerful capabilities for pattern matching, data extraction, and text transformation that, when orchestrated through intelligent scripting, can process log files more efficiently and comprehensively than manual analysis approaches.

Advanced Pattern Matching with Grep

Grep's pattern matching capabilities extend far beyond simple string searches, encompassing sophisticated regular expression techniques that enable identification of complex patterns, extraction of specific data elements, and filtering of log entries based on multiple criteria. Understanding how to leverage grep's advanced features enables creation of log analysis workflows that can identify subtle indicators of malicious activity while processing large volumes of data efficiently.

Regular expression mastery for security analysis requires understanding how to construct patterns that match security-relevant indicators while avoiding false positives that reduce analysis effectiveness. Security log analysis often involves identifying patterns that may appear in various formats, require case-insensitive matching, or need to account for variations in timestamp formats, IP address representations, and other data elements that appear differently across various log sources.

The construction of effective security-focused regular expressions requires understanding how attackers might attempt to evade detection through encoding, obfuscation, or variation techniques while ensuring that legitimate activities are not misidentified as threats. This balance between sensitivity and specificity becomes crucial when developing automated analysis systems that must operate reliably across diverse log sources and activity patterns.

Context-aware pattern matching enables identification of security events that depend on surrounding log entries for proper interpretation. Understanding how to use grep's context options effectively enables extraction of complete incident information while providing the situational awareness necessary for accurate threat assessment and investigation planning.

The implementation of context-aware matching requires understanding how security events often span multiple log entries and how to capture sufficient context to enable proper interpretation while avoiding excessive data collection that reduces analysis efficiency. This systematic approach enables comprehensive threat detection while maintaining analytical focus on relevant information.

Multi-file pattern correlation enables identification of related security events across different log sources, providing capabilities for detecting distributed attacks or coordinated activities that might not be apparent when analyzing individual log files in isolation. Understanding how to implement cross-file correlation enables creation of analysis workflows that provide comprehensive threat detection capabilities.

Performance optimization for large-scale log processing requires understanding how to use grep efficiently when processing gigabytes of log data while maintaining reasonable processing times and resource usage. This includes understanding how to optimize regular expressions, use appropriate grep options, and structure analysis workflows to maximize processing efficiency.

Sophisticated Data Extraction with Awk

Awk provides sophisticated programming capabilities that enable extraction, transformation, and analysis of structured log data while implementing complex logic for pattern recognition and data correlation. Understanding how to leverage awk's programming features enables creation of log analysis workflows that can process complex log formats, perform statistical analysis, and generate detailed reports that support security assessment and incident investigation activities.

Field-based data processing enables systematic extraction of specific information elements from structured log entries while handling variations in log format and data organization that are common across different systems and applications. Understanding how to implement robust field processing enables creation of analysis workflows that can adapt to different log formats while maintaining consistent data extraction and analysis capabilities.

The implementation of effective field processing requires understanding how different log formats organize information and how to handle variations in field ordering, delimiter usage, and data representation that can affect extraction reliability. This systematic approach enables consistent data processing across diverse log sources while maintaining analytical accuracy.

Statistical analysis capabilities enable calculation of frequency distributions, trend analysis, and anomaly detection that provide insights into normal system behavior patterns and identification of activities that deviate from established baselines. Understanding how to implement statistical analysis enables creation of monitoring systems that can identify subtle indicators of malicious activity while providing quantitative assessment of security posture.

Pattern recognition and classification capabilities enable identification of different types of security events based on log entry characteristics while implementing intelligent categorization that supports prioritized analysis and response activities. Understanding how to implement pattern classification enables creation of analysis workflows that can distinguish between different types of threats while providing appropriate context for incident response planning.

Advanced string manipulation and data transformation capabilities enable normalization of log data from different sources into consistent formats that support correlation and analysis activities. Understanding how to implement effective data transformation enables creation of analysis workflows that can process diverse log sources while maintaining analytical consistency and accuracy.

Time-based analysis and correlation capabilities enable identification of temporal patterns in security events while implementing sliding window analysis that can detect time-based attack signatures and coordinated activities. Understanding how to implement temporal analysis enables creation of monitoring systems that can identify sophisticated attack campaigns while providing comprehensive threat intelligence.

Stream Editing and Log Transformation with Sed

Sed provides powerful stream editing capabilities that enable real-time transformation of log data while implementing filtering, normalization, and formatting operations that support automated analysis workflows. Understanding how to leverage sed effectively enables creation of log processing pipelines that can handle diverse input formats while producing consistent, analyzable output that supports security monitoring and incident detection activities.

Real-time log preprocessing enables transformation of raw log data into standardized formats that support automated analysis while filtering out irrelevant information that might interfere with threat detection activities. Understanding how to implement effective preprocessing enables creation of analysis workflows that maximize signal-to-noise ratios while maintaining comprehensive coverage of security-relevant events.

The implementation of real-time preprocessing requires understanding how to identify relevant log entries, standardize data formats, and eliminate noise while preserving all information necessary for accurate threat detection and incident investigation. This systematic approach enables efficient analysis while maintaining comprehensive security coverage.

Format standardization capabilities enable processing of log data from diverse sources through consistent analysis workflows while handling variations in timestamp formats, field ordering, and data representation that are common across different systems and vendors. Understanding how to implement format standardization enables creation of unified analysis platforms that can process multiple log sources effectively.

Data anonymization and sanitization capabilities enable protection of sensitive information during log processing while maintaining analytical value for security monitoring and threat detection activities. Understanding how to implement appropriate anonymization enables creation of analysis workflows that support security requirements while respecting privacy and regulatory constraints.

Log enrichment and annotation capabilities enable addition of contextual information to log entries while implementing tagging and classification systems that support automated analysis and incident response activities. Understanding how to implement log enrichment enables creation of analysis workflows that provide comprehensive context for security events while supporting efficient threat assessment and response planning.

Integrated Text Processing Workflows

Combining grep, awk, and sed into sophisticated processing pipelines enables creation of comprehensive log analysis workflows that leverage the strengths of each tool while providing capabilities that exceed what any individual tool can accomplish. Understanding how to orchestrate these tools effectively enables creation of professional-quality log analysis systems that can handle enterprise-scale security monitoring requirements.

Pipeline architecture design enables creation of modular analysis workflows that can be easily modified, extended, and optimized for different log sources and analysis requirements. Understanding how to design effective pipeline architectures enables creation of maintainable analysis systems that can evolve to meet changing security requirements while maintaining reliable operation.

The implementation of effective pipeline architectures requires understanding how data flows between different processing stages and how to optimize performance while maintaining analytical accuracy and completeness. This systematic approach enables creation of scalable analysis systems that can handle large volumes of log data while providing timely threat detection capabilities.

Error handling and data validation capabilities ensure that analysis workflows continue operating effectively even when encountering malformed log entries or unexpected data formats while providing appropriate logging and alerting for conditions that require attention. Understanding how to implement robust error handling enables creation of reliable analysis systems that maintain operational effectiveness under diverse conditions.

Performance optimization and scalability considerations enable analysis workflows to handle enterprise-scale log volumes while maintaining reasonable processing times and resource usage. Understanding how to optimize text processing workflows enables creation of analysis systems that can scale to meet organizational requirements while maintaining analytical effectiveness.

Quality assurance and validation procedures ensure that analysis workflows produce accurate, reliable results while providing mechanisms for verifying analytical accuracy and identifying potential issues with processing logic or data interpretation. Understanding how to implement quality assurance enables creation of trustworthy analysis systems that provide reliable intelligence for security decision-making.

Scripting File Integrity Checks

File integrity monitoring represents a fundamental security control that provides detection capabilities for unauthorized file modifications, system compromises, and insider threats that might otherwise go undetected. Effective file integrity checking requires systematic approaches that can monitor critical files efficiently while distinguishing between legitimate administrative changes and potentially malicious modifications that require investigation and response.

Baseline Creation and Management

Establishing reliable baselines forms the foundation of effective file integrity monitoring by providing reference points against which future file states can be compared to detect changes. Understanding how to create and manage comprehensive baselines enables development of monitoring systems that can detect unauthorized modifications while minimizing false positives from legitimate administrative activities.

Critical file identification enables focused monitoring of files that have the greatest security significance while optimizing resource usage and avoiding excessive monitoring overhead that might interfere with system performance. Understanding how to identify critical files systematically enables creation of monitoring systems that provide comprehensive security coverage while maintaining efficient operation.

The identification of critical files requires understanding which system components are most likely to be targeted by attackers and which modifications would have the greatest impact on system security. This includes system binaries, configuration files, startup scripts, and other components that control system behavior and security settings.

Cryptographic hash implementation provides reliable mechanisms for detecting file modifications while enabling verification of file integrity across different time periods and system states. Understanding how to implement appropriate hashing algorithms enables creation of monitoring systems that can detect even subtle file modifications while maintaining reasonable performance characteristics.

Hash algorithm selection requires balancing security requirements with performance considerations while ensuring that chosen algorithms provide sufficient collision resistance for the intended monitoring applications. Modern cryptographic hash functions like SHA-256 provide excellent security properties while maintaining reasonable performance for most file integrity monitoring applications.

Baseline storage and management requires secure, tamper-resistant storage mechanisms that protect baseline data from unauthorized modification while providing efficient access for integrity checking operations. Understanding how to implement secure baseline storage enables creation of monitoring systems that maintain reliable reference data while protecting against compromise of the monitoring system itself.

Version control integration enables tracking of legitimate file changes while providing mechanisms for distinguishing between authorized modifications and potentially malicious changes. Understanding how to integrate version control capabilities enables creation of monitoring systems that can accommodate legitimate administrative activities while maintaining effective threat detection capabilities.

Change Detection and Analysis

Effective change detection requires systematic comparison of current file states against established baselines while implementing intelligent analysis that can distinguish between different types of modifications and assess their potential security significance. Understanding how to implement comprehensive change detection enables creation of monitoring systems that provide actionable security intelligence while minimizing false positive alerts.

Differential analysis capabilities enable identification of specific changes that have occurred to monitored files while providing detailed information about the nature and scope of detected modifications. Understanding how to implement differential analysis enables creation of monitoring systems that provide comprehensive change information necessary for security assessment and incident investigation.

The implementation of effective differential analysis requires understanding how to compare file states efficiently while providing sufficient detail about detected changes to support security decision-making. This includes identifying which portions of files have been modified, when changes occurred, and what types of modifications were made.

Change classification and prioritization enables monitoring systems to distinguish between different types of file modifications while providing appropriate urgency levels for different categories of changes. Understanding how to implement intelligent classification enables creation of monitoring systems that focus attention on the most critical security events while maintaining comprehensive coverage of potential threats.

Temporal correlation analysis enables identification of related file changes that occur within specific time windows while providing insights into coordinated modification activities that might indicate systematic attacks or unauthorized access. Understanding how to implement temporal correlation enables detection of sophisticated attack patterns while providing comprehensive threat intelligence.

Attribution and source analysis capabilities enable identification of the processes, users, or systems responsible for detected file changes while providing context that supports security assessment and incident response activities. Understanding how to implement attribution analysis enables creation of monitoring systems that provide actionable intelligence for threat investigation and response planning.

Advanced Integrity Monitoring Techniques

Beyond basic file modification detection, advanced integrity monitoring techniques provide capabilities for detecting sophisticated attack techniques while implementing proactive security measures that can prevent unauthorized modifications from occurring. Understanding how to implement advanced monitoring techniques enables creation of comprehensive security systems that provide both detective and preventive capabilities.

Real-time monitoring capabilities enable immediate detection of file modifications as they occur while providing opportunities for automated response to critical security events. Understanding how to implement real-time monitoring enables creation of systems that can respond rapidly to threats while providing comprehensive situational awareness of system security status.

The implementation of real-time monitoring requires understanding how to monitor file system events efficiently while managing resource usage and avoiding performance impact on monitored systems. This includes leveraging operating system features like inotify on Linux systems while implementing appropriate filtering and prioritization mechanisms.

Extended attribute monitoring enables detection of changes to file metadata, permissions, and other characteristics that might not be apparent through content-based integrity checking alone. Understanding how to implement extended attribute monitoring enables creation of comprehensive monitoring systems that detect all types of security-relevant file modifications.

Network-based integrity verification enables validation of file integrity across distributed systems while providing centralized monitoring capabilities that can detect coordinated attacks or systematic compromise activities. Understanding how to implement network-based verification enables creation of enterprise-scale monitoring systems that provide comprehensive security coverage.

Tamper-evident logging capabilities ensure that integrity monitoring activities themselves are protected against compromise while providing audit trails that support forensic investigation and compliance requirements. Understanding how to implement tamper-evident logging enables creation of monitoring systems that maintain their own integrity while providing reliable security intelligence.

Integration with Incident Response

Effective file integrity monitoring integrates seamlessly with incident response processes to ensure that detected changes trigger appropriate investigation and response activities while providing the information necessary for effective threat analysis and remediation planning. Understanding how to implement incident response integration enables creation of monitoring systems that provide not just detection capabilities but also support coordinated security response activities.

Automated alerting and escalation capabilities ensure that critical file modifications receive immediate attention while providing appropriate notification mechanisms for different types of security events. Understanding how to implement effective alerting enables creation of monitoring systems that provide timely threat notification while avoiding alert fatigue from excessive notifications.

Evidence preservation and forensic capabilities ensure that information about detected file modifications is captured and preserved in formats that support detailed investigation and legal proceedings if necessary. Understanding how to implement evidence preservation enables creation of monitoring systems that support comprehensive incident response while maintaining appropriate chain of custody for forensic evidence.

Response coordination and workflow integration enable monitoring systems to trigger appropriate incident response activities while providing mechanisms for coordinating response efforts across multiple security tools and personnel. Understanding how to implement response coordination enables creation of monitoring systems that support organizational incident response processes while providing effective threat detection capabilities.

Detecting Brute-Force Attempts from Auth Logs

Authentication log analysis provides critical capabilities for detecting unauthorized access attempts, identifying attack patterns, and assessing the effectiveness of access control mechanisms. Brute-force attacks represent one of the most common threats against authentication systems, making automated detection of these activities essential for maintaining effective security monitoring and incident response capabilities.

Authentication Log Structure and Analysis

Understanding authentication log formats and content enables development of comprehensive analysis workflows that can extract relevant security information while handling variations in log structure and content that are common across different systems and authentication mechanisms. Effective authentication log analysis requires systematic approaches that can identify attack patterns while distinguishing between legitimate authentication failures and malicious activities.

Log format standardization across different systems and authentication mechanisms enables creation of unified analysis workflows that can process authentication data from diverse sources while maintaining consistent detection capabilities. Understanding how to normalize authentication log data enables creation of analysis systems that provide comprehensive coverage while maintaining analytical consistency.

The implementation of log format standardization requires understanding how different systems record authentication events and how to transform diverse log formats into consistent structures that support automated analysis. This includes handling variations in timestamp formats, field organization, and data representation while preserving all security-relevant information.

Authentication event classification enables systematic categorization of different types of authentication activities while providing appropriate analysis techniques for each category of events. Understanding how to implement effective classification enables creation of analysis systems that can distinguish between different types of authentication threats while providing targeted detection capabilities.

User behavior pattern analysis enables identification of normal authentication patterns for different users and user types while providing baseline information that supports anomaly detection and threat identification. Understanding how to implement behavioral analysis enables creation of monitoring systems that can detect subtle indicators of compromise while minimizing false positives from legitimate user activities.

Geographic and temporal analysis capabilities enable identification of authentication patterns that might indicate compromise or abuse while providing context that supports threat assessment and investigation planning. Understanding how to implement location and time-based analysis enables creation of monitoring systems that can detect sophisticated attack techniques while providing comprehensive threat intelligence.

Brute-Force Attack Pattern Recognition

Brute-force attacks exhibit characteristic patterns that can be detected through systematic analysis of authentication logs while implementing intelligent algorithms that can distinguish between automated attacks and legitimate user activities. Understanding how to implement effective pattern recognition enables creation of detection systems that can identify brute-force attacks reliably while providing detailed information necessary for incident response and mitigation activities.

Frequency analysis capabilities enable detection of authentication attempts that exceed normal patterns while implementing sliding window analysis that can identify sustained attack activities over various time periods. Understanding how to implement frequency analysis enables creation of detection systems that can identify both rapid-fire attacks and slow, persistent attack campaigns.

The implementation of effective frequency analysis requires understanding how to establish appropriate thresholds that distinguish between normal authentication patterns and attack activities while accounting for legitimate variations in user behavior and system usage patterns. This systematic approach enables reliable attack detection while minimizing false positive alerts.

Source analysis and correlation enables identification of attack campaigns that originate from multiple sources while providing insights into attack coordination and distribution that support threat assessment and response planning. Understanding how to implement source correlation enables creation of detection systems that can identify sophisticated, distributed attack campaigns.

Target analysis capabilities enable identification of accounts that are being targeted by attack activities while providing prioritized intelligence that supports focused security response and account protection activities. Understanding how to implement target analysis enables creation of detection systems that provide actionable intelligence for threat mitigation and user protection.

Success rate analysis enables assessment of attack effectiveness while identifying attacks that achieve partial success and might indicate compromised accounts or credential theft. Understanding how to implement success rate analysis enables creation of detection systems that can identify successful attacks while providing early warning of potential compromise activities.

Advanced Threat Detection Techniques

Beyond basic brute-force detection, advanced techniques enable identification of sophisticated attack methods that might evade traditional detection approaches while providing comprehensive coverage of authentication-related threats. Understanding how to implement advanced detection techniques enables creation of monitoring systems that can identify evolving attack methods while maintaining effective threat detection capabilities.

Password spray detection enables identification of attacks that target multiple accounts with common passwords while avoiding the high frequency patterns that characterize traditional brute-force attacks. Understanding how to implement password spray detection enables creation of monitoring systems that can identify sophisticated attack techniques while providing comprehensive threat coverage.

The implementation of password spray detection requires understanding how these attacks differ from traditional brute-force approaches and how to identify attack patterns that span multiple accounts and extended time periods. This systematic approach enables detection of subtle attack techniques while maintaining analytical accuracy.

Credential stuffing detection enables identification of attacks that use compromised credentials from other breaches while implementing analysis techniques that can distinguish between legitimate authentication activities and automated attack tools. Understanding how to implement credential stuffing detection enables creation of monitoring systems that can identify attacks using valid credentials.

Account enumeration detection enables identification of reconnaissance activities that attempt to identify valid user accounts while providing early warning of potential attack preparation activities. Understanding how to implement enumeration detection enables creation of monitoring systems that can detect preliminary attack activities while providing opportunities for proactive threat mitigation.

Behavioral anomaly detection enables identification of authentication patterns that deviate from normal user behavior while implementing machine learning techniques that can adapt to changing user behavior patterns and emerging attack techniques. Understanding how to implement behavioral detection enables creation of adaptive monitoring systems that can identify novel attack approaches.

Automated Response and Mitigation

Effective brute-force detection systems integrate automated response capabilities that can implement immediate mitigation measures while providing escalation paths for situations that require human intervention. Understanding how to implement automated response enables creation of detection systems that can respond rapidly to threats while maintaining appropriate oversight and control mechanisms.

Account lockout automation enables immediate protection of targeted accounts while implementing intelligent lockout policies that balance security protection with user productivity requirements. Understanding how to implement automated lockout enables creation of responsive protection systems that can prevent successful attacks while minimizing impact on legitimate users.

IP blocking and rate limiting capabilities enable implementation of network-level protections that can prevent attack continuation while providing mechanisms for managing legitimate traffic and avoiding excessive blocking of legitimate users. Understanding how to implement network-based protections enables creation of comprehensive defense systems that provide multiple layers of attack prevention.

Alert escalation and notification systems ensure that detected attacks receive appropriate attention while providing detailed information necessary for investigation and response planning. Understanding how to implement effective notification systems enables creation of detection systems that support coordinated incident response while providing timely threat intelligence.

Writing a Lightweight Intrusion Detection Script

Creating a comprehensive intrusion detection system through Bash scripting demonstrates advanced automation capabilities while providing practical security monitoring that can complement commercial security tools or serve as standalone monitoring solutions for resource-constrained environments. A well-designed intrusion detection script integrates multiple detection techniques while providing flexible configuration and comprehensive reporting capabilities.

System Architecture and Design Philosophy

Effective intrusion detection systems require careful architectural design that balances detection capability with system performance while providing modular structures that can be easily modified and extended as requirements evolve. Understanding how to design scalable detection architectures enables creation of monitoring systems that can grow to meet organizational needs while maintaining reliable operation.

Modular detection framework design enables creation of intrusion detection systems that can incorporate different detection techniques through standardized interfaces while providing centralized coordination and reporting capabilities. Understanding how to implement modular architectures enables creation of flexible systems that can adapt to different environments and requirements while maintaining consistent operation.

The implementation of modular detection frameworks requires understanding how to separate different detection functions while maintaining appropriate communication and coordination between system components. This systematic approach enables creation of maintainable systems that can evolve to incorporate new detection techniques while preserving existing functionality.

Event correlation and analysis capabilities enable identification of complex attack patterns that span multiple detection domains while providing comprehensive threat assessment that supports effective incident response. Understanding how to implement event correlation enables creation of detection systems that provide intelligence rather than just individual alerts.

Performance optimization and resource management ensure that detection systems operate efficiently while maintaining comprehensive security coverage without imposing excessive load on monitored systems. Understanding how to optimize detection performance enables creation of systems that provide effective monitoring while respecting operational constraints.

Scalability considerations enable detection systems to handle increasing data volumes and expanded monitoring scope while maintaining detection effectiveness and system reliability. Understanding how to design scalable systems enables creation of monitoring solutions that can grow with organizational requirements while maintaining consistent operation.

Multi-Vector Detection Implementation

Comprehensive intrusion detection requires monitoring multiple attack vectors simultaneously while implementing detection techniques that can identify different types of threats and attack methods. Understanding how to implement multi-vector detection enables creation of comprehensive monitoring systems that provide thorough security coverage while maintaining analytical focus on relevant threats.

Network-based detection capabilities enable identification of malicious network activities including port scans, denial of service attacks, and suspicious communication patterns that might indicate compromise or attack activities. Understanding how to implement network detection enables creation of systems that can monitor network-level threats while providing detailed information for investigation and response.

The implementation of network-based detection requires understanding how to monitor network traffic patterns efficiently while identifying activities that deviate from normal communication patterns and might indicate malicious activity. This includes monitoring connection patterns, traffic volumes, and communication destinations while avoiding excessive resource usage.

Host-based detection capabilities enable identification of suspicious activities on individual systems including unauthorized file modifications, process anomalies, and privilege escalation attempts. Understanding how to implement host-based detection enables creation of comprehensive monitoring systems that can detect insider threats and local compromise activities.

Application-level detection capabilities enable identification of attacks targeting specific applications and services while implementing detection techniques that can identify application-specific attack methods and vulnerabilities. Understanding how to implement application detection enables creation of specialized monitoring that can protect critical applications while providing detailed threat intelligence.

Log-based detection integration enables correlation of events from multiple log sources while implementing analysis techniques that can identify attack patterns that span multiple systems and time periods. Understanding how to implement log correlation enables creation of comprehensive detection systems that can identify sophisticated attack campaigns.

Real-Time Monitoring and Analysis

Real-time detection capabilities enable immediate identification of security threats while providing opportunities for automated response that can prevent or limit attack success. Understanding how to implement real-time monitoring enables creation of responsive detection systems that can adapt to dynamic threat environments while maintaining comprehensive security coverage.

Stream processing implementation enables analysis of security events as they occur while providing low-latency detection that can identify time-sensitive threats before they cause significant damage. Understanding how to implement stream processing enables creation of detection systems that provide immediate threat awareness while maintaining analytical accuracy.

The implementation of effective stream processing requires understanding how to handle continuous data streams efficiently while maintaining detection accuracy and avoiding resource exhaustion from sustained high-volume events. This systematic approach enables creation of reliable real-time monitoring that can handle diverse operational conditions.

Event buffering and queue management capabilities enable detection systems to handle variable event volumes while maintaining processing reliability and avoiding data loss during high-activity periods. Understanding how to implement effective buffering enables creation of robust detection systems that maintain reliable operation under diverse conditions.

Threshold management and adaptive detection enable monitoring systems to adjust their sensitivity based on current threat levels and system activity patterns while maintaining effective threat detection across different operational conditions. Understanding how to implement adaptive detection enables creation of intelligent monitoring systems that can optimize their performance automatically.

Alert Management and Response Integration

Effective intrusion detection systems implement comprehensive alert management that provides appropriate prioritization, correlation, and escalation while integrating seamlessly with incident response processes. Understanding how to implement effective alert management enables creation of detection systems that provide actionable intelligence while supporting coordinated security response activities.

Alert prioritization and classification enable detection systems to distinguish between different types of threats while providing appropriate urgency levels that support efficient allocation of security resources. Understanding how to implement intelligent prioritization enables creation of detection systems that focus attention on the most critical threats while maintaining comprehensive security coverage.

The implementation of effective alert prioritization requires understanding how different types of security events relate to organizational risk tolerance and how to assign appropriate priority levels that support effective incident response while avoiding alert fatigue from excessive notifications.

Correlation and aggregation capabilities prevent alert flooding by combining related security events into comprehensive notifications while providing detailed information about the scope and nature of detected activities. Understanding how to implement alert correlation enables creation of detection systems that provide clear, actionable intelligence while avoiding information overload.

Escalation and notification systems ensure that critical security events receive appropriate attention while providing multiple communication channels and escalation paths that accommodate different availability patterns and organizational structures. Understanding how to implement effective notification systems enables creation of detection systems that support reliable incident response while maintaining operational flexibility.

Integration with external security tools enables detection systems to share threat intelligence and coordinate response activities with other security infrastructure while providing comprehensive security coverage that leverages multiple detection and response capabilities. Understanding how to implement tool integration enables creation of detection systems that serve as components in comprehensive security operations centers.

Conclusion

This chapter has established comprehensive automation capabilities for log analysis and incident detection that enable systematic processing of security data while providing intelligent threat detection and response coordination. From advanced text processing automation and file integrity monitoring to sophisticated brute-force detection and comprehensive intrusion detection systems, you've developed skills that address critical aspects of security monitoring while demonstrating advanced automation techniques that provide immediate operational value.

The progression from individual analysis tools to integrated detection frameworks demonstrates how fundamental text processing capabilities can be combined with intelligent logic to create sophisticated security monitoring solutions. The techniques covered in this chapter—automated log parsing, pattern recognition, anomaly detection, and intelligent alerting—represent core competencies that enable effective security operations at enterprise scale while providing the flexibility and customization capabilities that commercial solutions often lack.

The intrusion detection system developed in the final section provides a practical template for creating comprehensive security monitoring that can adapt to various organizational requirements while maintaining professional standards for performance, accuracy, and integration with existing security infrastructure. This system demonstrates how individual detection techniques combine to create monitoring capabilities that provide comprehensive threat coverage while maintaining operational efficiency and reliability.

The automation skills developed in this chapter enable systematic processing of security data and intelligent threat detection that would otherwise require substantial manual effort while providing more comprehensive and consistent results than traditional manual analysis approaches. More importantly, these automation capabilities enable security teams to focus their expertise on threat investigation, response coordination, and strategic security initiatives while delegating routine monitoring and analysis tasks to reliable automated systems.

Moving forward, the log analysis and detection automation capabilities established in this chapter provide the foundation for more advanced security automation projects including comprehensive security operations center automation, advanced threat hunting systems, and integrated incident response platforms. The patterns and practices demonstrated here—intelligent data processing, multi-source correlation, adaptive detection algorithms, and comprehensive reporting—will serve as templates for all future security automation development while ensuring that your tools maintain the reliability and effectiveness required for cybersecurity operations.

The investment you've made in understanding these log analysis and detection automation techniques will pay dividends throughout your cybersecurity career as you encounter new challenges that require systematic data processing and intelligent threat detection capabilities. With these capabilities firmly established, you're ready to explore more advanced automation topics that build upon this monitoring foundation while addressing other critical areas of cybersecurity operations such as threat hunting, incident response orchestration, and security operations center automation that leverage these fundamental analysis and detection skills in increasingly sophisticated ways.

Chapter 5: Bash in Offensive Security

Offensive security testing represents a critical component of comprehensive cybersecurity programs, enabling organizations to identify vulnerabilities and assess security controls through authorized penetration testing, red team exercises, and security assessments. The ability to develop, deploy, and execute effective attack techniques provides essential insights into security posture while validating the effectiveness of defensive measures. However, the development of offensive capabilities requires careful consideration of legal, ethical, and professional boundaries to ensure that security testing activities achieve their intended objectives while maintaining appropriate safeguards and professional standards.

Bash scripting provides powerful capabilities for developing offensive security tools and techniques that leverage the ubiquity and flexibility of shell environments while enabling rapid development and deployment of custom attack tools. The combination of Bash's text processing capabilities, system integration features, and network communication tools creates opportunities for developing sophisticated attack techniques that can adapt to different target environments while maintaining stealth and reliability characteristics essential for effective penetration testing.

This chapter explores the development of offensive security capabilities through advanced Bash scripting techniques while maintaining strict focus on legitimate security testing applications. All techniques covered in this chapter are intended exclusively for authorized penetration testing, red team exercises, and security research conducted within appropriate legal and ethical frameworks. The concepts and tools presented here should only be used by security professionals conducting authorized testing activities with explicit permission from system owners and within clearly defined scope boundaries.

The progression through this chapter builds from fundamental payload development concepts to sophisticated attack automation frameworks that demonstrate professional-level offensive capabilities. Each section emphasizes not only technical implementation but also the operational considerations, detection avoidance techniques, and professional practices that distinguish legitimate security testing from malicious activities. Understanding these distinctions is essential for security professionals who must develop effective testing capabilities while maintaining ethical standards and legal compliance.

Crafting Payloads and Obfuscating with Bash

Payload development represents a fundamental skill in offensive security testing, enabling creation of custom attack tools that can adapt to specific target environments while achieving testing objectives efficiently. Effective payload development requires understanding how to create reliable, flexible attack code while implementing obfuscation techniques that can evade detection systems and demonstrate the effectiveness of security controls under realistic attack conditions.

Fundamental Payload Development Principles

Effective payload development requires systematic approaches that balance functionality, reliability, and stealth while ensuring that testing tools achieve their intended objectives without causing unintended damage or disruption. Understanding fundamental development principles enables creation of professional-quality testing tools that provide accurate assessment of security posture while maintaining appropriate safeguards for authorized testing activities.

Code reliability and error handling form critical components of professional payload development because testing tools must operate consistently across diverse target environments while providing predictable results that support accurate security assessment. Understanding how to implement robust error handling enables creation of payloads that can adapt to unexpected conditions while maintaining operational effectiveness and providing detailed feedback about testing activities.

The implementation of reliable payload code requires understanding how target systems might vary in their configurations, security controls, and operational characteristics while designing attack tools that can handle these variations gracefully. This systematic approach enables creation of testing tools that provide consistent results across different testing scenarios while maintaining appropriate operational security characteristics.

Modularity and reusability principles enable development of payload components that can be combined and reconfigured for different testing scenarios while maintaining code quality and reducing development overhead for complex testing campaigns. Understanding how to implement modular payload design enables creation of flexible testing frameworks that can adapt to diverse engagement requirements while maintaining professional development standards.

Stealth and evasion considerations require careful attention to how payloads interact with target systems and security controls while implementing techniques that can demonstrate the effectiveness of defensive measures under realistic attack conditions. Understanding how to implement appropriate stealth techniques enables creation of testing tools that provide accurate assessment of detection capabilities while maintaining realistic attack characteristics.

Documentation and version control practices ensure that payload development activities are properly documented and that testing tools can be maintained and improved over time while providing appropriate audit trails for professional testing activities. Understanding how to implement proper development practices enables creation of maintainable testing capabilities that support ongoing security assessment activities.

Advanced Obfuscation Techniques

Obfuscation techniques enable testing of detection systems and security controls by implementing attack methods that attempt to evade automated analysis while demonstrating potential gaps in security monitoring capabilities. Understanding how to implement various obfuscation approaches enables development of testing tools that can assess the effectiveness of security controls under conditions that simulate real-world attack techniques.

String obfuscation and encoding techniques enable creation of payloads that can evade signature-based detection systems while maintaining functional effectiveness for authorized testing activities. Understanding how to implement string obfuscation enables development of testing tools that can demonstrate potential weaknesses in content-based security controls while providing insights into detection system effectiveness.

The implementation of effective string obfuscation requires understanding how detection systems analyze content and how various encoding, and transformation techniques can affect detection accuracy while maintaining payload functionality. This systematic approach enables creation of testing tools that provide accurate assessment of detection capabilities while demonstrating realistic attack techniques.

Code structure obfuscation enables testing of behavioral analysis systems by implementing attack techniques that use non-standard coding patterns while maintaining functional effectiveness. Understanding how to implement structural obfuscation enables development of testing tools that can assess the effectiveness of advanced detection systems while providing insights into behavioral analysis capabilities.

Dynamic code generation techniques enable creation of payloads that modify their behavior or structure during execution while maintaining testing effectiveness and providing assessment of adaptive security controls. Understanding how to implement dynamic techniques enables development of sophisticated testing tools that can demonstrate advanced attack methods while providing comprehensive security assessment capabilities.

Anti-analysis techniques enable testing of security research and incident response capabilities by implementing methods that can complicate analysis activities while demonstrating potential challenges that defenders might face during real security incidents. Understanding how to implement anti-analysis techniques enables development of realistic testing scenarios that provide comprehensive assessment of defensive capabilities.

Payload Delivery and Execution Strategies

Effective payload delivery requires understanding how to deploy testing tools through various vectors while maintaining operational security and achieving testing objectives efficiently. Understanding different delivery strategies enables development of comprehensive testing approaches that can assess multiple attack vectors while providing accurate assessment of overall security posture.

File-based delivery mechanisms enable testing of endpoint security controls and user awareness training effectiveness by implementing attack techniques that leverage various file formats and delivery methods. Understanding how to implement file-based delivery enables development of testing scenarios that can assess the effectiveness of email security, endpoint protection, and user security awareness programs.

The implementation of effective file-based delivery requires understanding how different file formats can be used for attack purposes and how security controls might detect or prevent malicious file execution while designing testing approaches that provide accurate assessment of defensive capabilities.

Network-based delivery techniques enable testing of network security controls and monitoring capabilities by implementing attack methods that leverage network communication channels for payload delivery and execution. Understanding how to implement network-based delivery enables development of testing scenarios that can assess network security effectiveness while providing insights into detection and prevention capabilities.

Memory-based execution techniques enable testing of advanced endpoint protection systems by implementing attack methods that minimize forensic evidence while maintaining testing effectiveness. Understanding how to implement memory-based techniques enables development of sophisticated testing approaches that can assess the effectiveness of advanced security controls while providing realistic attack scenarios.

Persistence mechanisms enable testing of long-term security monitoring and incident response capabilities by implementing techniques that can maintain access across system restarts and security updates. Understanding how to implement persistence testing enables development of comprehensive security assessments that evaluate ongoing monitoring effectiveness while providing insights into long-term security posture.

Environmental Adaptation and Targeting

Professional penetration testing requires attack tools that can adapt to different target environments while maintaining effectiveness across diverse system configurations and security implementations. Understanding how to develop adaptive payloads enables creation of testing tools that provide consistent results while accommodating the variety of systems and configurations encountered in real-world testing scenarios.

System fingerprinting and reconnaissance integration enable payloads to gather information about target environments while adapting their behavior based on discovered system characteristics. Understanding how to implement adaptive reconnaissance enables development of intelligent testing tools that can optimize their approach based on target system properties while maintaining appropriate operational security.

The implementation of effective system adaptation requires understanding how to gather information about target systems safely while using this information to optimize attack approaches and increase testing effectiveness. This systematic approach enables creation of testing tools that provide comprehensive security assessment while maintaining realistic attack characteristics.

Operating system and architecture detection enables payloads to adapt their behavior based on target system characteristics while maintaining compatibility across different platforms and configurations. Understanding how to implement cross-platform adaptation enables development of versatile testing tools that can operate effectively in diverse environments while providing consistent testing results.

Security control detection and evasion enable testing tools to identify and adapt to various security measures while demonstrating potential weaknesses in defensive implementations. Understanding how to implement security control assessment enables development of testing approaches that provide comprehensive evaluation of defensive effectiveness while maintaining realistic attack scenarios.

Application and service targeting enables development of specialized payloads that can test specific applications or services while providing focused assessment of particular security controls or configurations. Understanding how to implement targeted testing enables development of specialized assessment capabilities that can provide detailed evaluation of specific security components while maintaining overall testing effectiveness.

Automating Social Engineering Payload Delivery

Social engineering attacks represent significant threats that combine technical attack methods with psychological manipulation to achieve unauthorized access or information disclosure. Automating social engineering payload delivery enables comprehensive testing of human factors in security while providing scalable approaches for assessing organizational vulnerability to these hybrid attack techniques that combine technology with human psychology.

Social Engineering Framework Development

Effective social engineering automation requires systematic frameworks that can coordinate technical and psychological attack elements while maintaining appropriate boundaries for authorized testing activities. Understanding how to develop comprehensive social engineering frameworks enables creation of testing capabilities that can assess human factors in security while maintaining professional standards and ethical boundaries.

Target research and profiling automation enables systematic gathering of information about target individuals or organizations while providing intelligence that can be used to craft convincing social engineering attacks. Understanding how to implement automated research capabilities enables development of testing frameworks that can assess the effectiveness of information security awareness programs while providing realistic assessment of social engineering vulnerabilities.

The implementation of automated target research requires understanding how to gather publicly available information efficiently while respecting privacy boundaries and legal limitations that apply to authorized security testing activities. This systematic approach enables creation of testing capabilities that provide realistic social engineering scenarios while maintaining appropriate professional and legal standards.

Communication channel automation enables testing of various social engineering delivery methods including email, social media, messaging platforms, and other communication channels that attackers might use to deliver social engineering attacks. Understanding how to implement multi-channel delivery enables development of comprehensive testing approaches that can assess organizational vulnerability across different communication platforms.

Campaign management and coordination capabilities enable orchestration of complex social engineering testing scenarios while providing appropriate tracking and documentation of testing activities. Understanding how to implement campaign management enables development of sophisticated testing frameworks that can coordinate multiple attack vectors while maintaining detailed records of testing activities for analysis and reporting.

Template and content generation automation enables creation of convincing social engineering content while providing scalable approaches for developing testing materials that can adapt to different target profiles and scenarios. Understanding how to implement content automation enables development of efficient testing frameworks that can generate realistic social engineering scenarios while maintaining professional testing standards.

Phishing and Email-Based Attack Automation

Email-based social engineering represents one of the most common attack vectors, making comprehensive testing of email security controls and user awareness essential components of security assessment programs. Understanding how to automate phishing testing enables development of scalable assessment capabilities that can evaluate both technical controls and human factors in email security.

Email template development and customization enable creation of convincing phishing emails that can test user awareness and email security controls while providing realistic assessment of organizational vulnerability to email-based attacks. Understanding how to develop effective email templates enables creation of testing scenarios that provide accurate assessment of phishing susceptibility while maintaining appropriate testing boundaries.

The development of effective phishing templates requires understanding how attackers craft convincing emails and how various design elements, content strategies, and technical implementations can affect the success of social engineering attacks while ensuring that testing activities remain within appropriate boundaries for authorized security assessment.

Personalization and targeting automation enable creation of customized phishing emails that leverage target research information while providing scalable approaches for developing convincing attack scenarios. Understanding how to implement personalization automation enables development of sophisticated testing capabilities that can assess the effectiveness of targeted social engineering attacks while maintaining efficient testing operations.

Email delivery and tracking automation enable systematic deployment of phishing testing campaigns while providing detailed monitoring of user responses and email security control effectiveness. Understanding how to implement delivery automation enables development of comprehensive testing frameworks that can assess both technical and human factors in email security while providing detailed analysis of testing results.

Link and attachment payload integration enables testing of various attack vectors through phishing emails while providing assessment of how users and security controls respond to different types of malicious content. Understanding how to implement payload integration enables development of comprehensive phishing testing that can assess multiple attack vectors while providing detailed evaluation of defensive effectiveness.

Web-Based Social Engineering Automation

Web-based social engineering attacks leverage malicious websites, compromised legitimate sites, and web application vulnerabilities to deliver attack payloads while taking advantage of user trust and familiarity with web browsing activities. Understanding how to automate web-based social engineering testing enables comprehensive assessment of web security controls and user awareness regarding web-based threats.

Malicious website creation and hosting automation enable development of convincing fake websites that can test user awareness and web security controls while providing realistic assessment of organizational vulnerability to web-based social engineering attacks. Understanding how to implement website automation enables creation of testing scenarios that provide comprehensive evaluation of web-based attack susceptibility while maintaining appropriate testing standards.

The implementation of automated malicious website creation requires understanding how to develop convincing website replicas and how to implement various attack techniques through web interfaces while ensuring that testing activities remain within appropriate boundaries and do not cause unintended harm or disruption.

Credential harvesting and form manipulation automation enable testing of how users and security controls respond to fake login pages and malicious web forms while providing assessment of awareness training effectiveness and technical control capabilities. Understanding how to implement credential harvesting testing enables development of comprehensive web security assessment while maintaining appropriate ethical boundaries.

Browser exploitation and client-side attack automation enable testing of web browser security and endpoint protection effectiveness while providing assessment of how technical controls respond to various web-based attack techniques. Understanding how to implement browser-based testing enables development of sophisticated web security assessment capabilities while maintaining professional testing standards.

Traffic analysis and user behavior tracking enable assessment of how users interact with malicious websites while providing insights into the effectiveness of security awareness training and technical controls. Understanding how to implement behavior analysis enables development of comprehensive testing frameworks that can assess both technical and human factors in web security while providing detailed evaluation of defensive effectiveness.

Multi-Vector Campaign Coordination

Sophisticated social engineering attacks often combine multiple attack vectors and communication channels to increase their effectiveness while evading detection systems that might identify individual attack components. Understanding how to coordinate multi-vector social engineering campaigns enables development of comprehensive testing scenarios that can assess organizational resilience against coordinated attack campaigns.

Cross-platform attack coordination enables testing scenarios that leverage multiple communication channels and attack vectors while providing assessment of how security controls and user awareness programs respond to coordinated attacks. Understanding how to implement cross-platform coordination enables development of sophisticated testing capabilities that provide realistic assessment of advanced social engineering threats.

The implementation of effective multi-vector coordination requires understanding how different attack components can be synchronized and how the combination of multiple attack vectors can increase overall attack effectiveness while ensuring that testing activities remain within appropriate scope and boundaries for authorized security assessment.

Timing and sequencing automation enable optimization of attack delivery timing while providing assessment of how temporal factors affect the success of social engineering attacks and the effectiveness of defensive responses. Understanding how to implement timing coordination enables development of testing frameworks that can assess the impact of attack timing on defensive effectiveness while providing comprehensive evaluation of security controls.

Intelligence gathering and feedback integration enable dynamic adjustment of social engineering campaigns based on target responses and defensive actions while providing continuous optimization of testing effectiveness. Understanding how to implement adaptive campaigns enables development of sophisticated testing capabilities that can respond to defensive measures while maintaining realistic attack characteristics.

Campaign analysis and reporting automation enable comprehensive evaluation of multi-vector social engineering testing results while providing detailed assessment of organizational vulnerability and defensive effectiveness across multiple attack vectors. Understanding how to implement comprehensive analysis enables development of testing frameworks that provide actionable intelligence for security improvement while maintaining professional reporting standards.

Building Bash Reverse Shell Scripts

Reverse shell development represents a fundamental skill in penetration testing that enables establishment of command-and-control capabilities during authorized security assessments. Understanding how to develop reliable, feature-rich reverse shell implementations enables creation of testing tools that can maintain persistent access for comprehensive security evaluation while demonstrating potential post-exploitation capabilities that attackers might achieve.

Reverse Shell Architecture and Design

Effective reverse shell implementation requires careful architectural design that balances functionality, reliability, and stealth while providing capabilities necessary for comprehensive security testing. Understanding fundamental design principles enables development of reverse shell tools that can operate effectively in diverse target environments while maintaining appropriate operational security characteristics for authorized testing activities.

Connection establishment and maintenance mechanisms form the core of reliable reverse shell implementations by providing robust communication channels between compromised systems and testing infrastructure. Understanding how to implement reliable connection handling enables development of reverse shells that can maintain operational effectiveness across varying network conditions while providing consistent command and control capabilities.

The implementation of effective connection handling requires understanding how network communication can be disrupted and how to implement retry mechanisms, error handling, and failover capabilities that enable reverse shells to maintain functionality under adverse conditions while providing reliable testing capabilities.

Communication protocol design and implementation enable secure, efficient exchange of commands and data between reverse shell clients and command and control servers while implementing appropriate obfuscation and encryption that can evade detection systems. Understanding how to implement effective communication protocols enables development of sophisticated reverse shell capabilities that provide comprehensive testing while maintaining operational security.

Command execution and environment management capabilities enable reverse shells to provide comprehensive system access while implementing appropriate safety mechanisms that prevent unintended damage during authorized testing activities. Understanding how to implement safe command execution enables development of testing tools that provide necessary access while maintaining appropriate safeguards for professional security testing.

Process management and resource utilization optimization ensure that reverse shells operate efficiently while minimizing their impact on target system performance and avoiding detection through resource monitoring systems. Understanding how to implement efficient resource management enables development of reverse shells that provide necessary capabilities while maintaining appropriate stealth characteristics.

Advanced Communication Techniques

Professional reverse shell implementations require sophisticated communication capabilities that can adapt to different network environments while evading detection systems and maintaining reliable operation across diverse deployment scenarios. Understanding advanced communication techniques enables development of reverse shell tools that provide comprehensive testing capabilities while demonstrating realistic attack characteristics.

Encrypted communication implementation enables protection of command-and-control traffic while preventing network monitoring systems from intercepting sensitive testing activities or identifying reverse shell communications. Understanding how to implement encryption enables development of secure reverse shell capabilities that provide realistic assessment of network monitoring effectiveness while maintaining operational security for authorized testing.

The implementation of effective encryption requires understanding how to balance security with performance while ensuring that encrypted communications can operate efficiently across different network conditions and do not create excessive overhead that might affect reverse shell reliability or performance.

Protocol tunneling and encapsulation techniques enable reverse shell traffic to traverse network security controls while providing assessment of how security devices respond to various tunneling methods and protocol manipulation techniques. Understanding how to implement tunneling enables development of reverse shell capabilities that can test network security effectiveness while providing comprehensive access for security assessment.

Multi-channel communication and redundancy capabilities enable reverse shells to maintain connectivity through multiple communication paths while providing resilience against network disruptions and security control interventions. Understanding how to implement redundant communications enables development of robust reverse shell capabilities that can maintain operational effectiveness under adverse conditions.

Bandwidth optimization and traffic shaping enable reverse shells to operate efficiently across limited network connections while implementing communication patterns that can evade traffic analysis and bandwidth monitoring systems. Understanding how to implement traffic optimization enables development of efficient reverse shell capabilities that can operate effectively in resource-constrained environments while maintaining appropriate stealth characteristics.

Interactive Shell Enhancement

Basic reverse shell implementations provide limited command execution capabilities, but professional penetration testing requires enhanced interactive shells that provide comprehensive system access and administrative capabilities. Understanding how to implement interactive shell enhancements enables development of sophisticated testing tools that provide complete system access for thorough security assessment.

Terminal emulation and interactive command processing enable reverse shells to provide full interactive terminal access while supporting complex command sequences, interactive applications, and advanced system administration activities. Understanding how to implement terminal emulation enables development of reverse shells that provide comprehensive system access for detailed security testing while maintaining user-friendly operation.

The implementation of effective terminal emulation requires understanding how different terminal types and shell environments operate while ensuring that reverse shell implementations can provide consistent interactive access across different target systems and configurations.

File transfer and data exfiltration capabilities enable bidirectional file transfer between compromised systems and testing infrastructure while providing secure, efficient methods for gathering evidence and deploying additional testing tools. Understanding how to implement file transfer capabilities enables development of comprehensive reverse shell tools that support complex testing scenarios while providing necessary data movement capabilities.

Process monitoring and system information gathering automation enable reverse shells to collect detailed information about target systems while providing intelligence necessary for comprehensive security assessment and additional testing activities. Understanding how to implement system monitoring enables development of reverse shells that provide valuable intelligence while maintaining efficient operation.

Privilege escalation and lateral movement integration enable reverse shells to leverage additional attack techniques while providing comprehensive assessment of security controls and demonstrating potential attack progression paths. Understanding how to implement privilege escalation capabilities enables development of sophisticated testing tools that can assess comprehensive security posture while providing realistic attack scenarios.

Persistence and Evasion Mechanisms

Professional reverse shell implementations must include capabilities for maintaining access across system restarts and security updates while evading detection systems that might identify and remove reverse shell components. Understanding persistence and evasion techniques enables development of comprehensive testing tools that can assess long-term security monitoring effectiveness while providing realistic assessment of advanced attack techniques.

Persistence mechanism implementation enables reverse shells to maintain access across various system events while providing assessment of how security controls detect and respond to persistence techniques. Understanding how to implement persistence enables development of testing tools that can assess long-term security monitoring while providing comprehensive evaluation of defensive capabilities.

The implementation of effective persistence requires understanding how different operating systems handle startup processes and how various persistence techniques can be detected by security controls while ensuring that testing activities remain within appropriate boundaries for authorized security assessment.

Anti-forensics and log evasion techniques enable reverse shells to minimize their forensic footprint while providing assessment of how incident response and forensic analysis capabilities can detect sophisticated attack techniques. Understanding how to implement anti-forensics capabilities enables development of testing tools that provide realistic assessment of detection and analysis capabilities while maintaining appropriate operational security.

Process hiding and memory-only execution techniques enable reverse shells to evade host-based security controls while providing assessment of advanced endpoint protection capabilities. Understanding how to implement process hiding enables development of sophisticated testing tools that can assess the effectiveness of advanced security controls while providing comprehensive security evaluation.

Dynamic adaptation and polymorphic capabilities enable reverse shells to modify their behavior and characteristics while maintaining operational effectiveness and evading signature-based detection systems. Understanding how to implement adaptive techniques enables development of advanced testing tools that can assess the effectiveness of various detection methods while providing sophisticated security assessment capabilities.

Chaining Bash with Netcat, Curl, and Wget

The integration of Bash scripting with powerful networking tools like Netcat, Curl, and Wget creates sophisticated automation capabilities that enable complex penetration testing scenarios while providing flexible, efficient approaches for network communication, data transfer, and service interaction. Understanding how to chain these tools effectively enables development of comprehensive testing frameworks that can address diverse attack scenarios while maintaining professional testing standards.

Netcat Integration and Network Communication

Netcat provides fundamental networking capabilities that, when combined with Bash scripting, enable development of sophisticated network-based testing tools and communication frameworks. Understanding how to integrate Netcat effectively enables creation of versatile testing capabilities that can handle diverse network communication requirements while providing reliable, efficient network operations for security testing activities.

Connection establishment and management through Netcat integration enable Bash scripts to create and maintain network connections for various testing purposes including port scanning, service interaction, and data transfer activities. Understanding how to implement connection management enables development of testing tools that can handle complex network communication requirements while providing reliable operation across diverse network environments.

The implementation of effective Netcat integration requires understanding how to manage connection states, handle network errors, and implement appropriate error recovery mechanisms that enable testing tools to operate reliably across different network conditions while maintaining operational effectiveness for security testing activities.

Port scanning and service enumeration automation through Netcat integration enable development of flexible scanning tools that can adapt their approach based on target characteristics while providing detailed information about discovered services and network configurations. Understanding how to implement scanning automation enables creation of versatile reconnaissance tools that can provide comprehensive network assessment while maintaining efficient operation.

Data transfer and file manipulation capabilities through Netcat integration enable secure, efficient transfer of files and data during testing activities while providing mechanisms for deploying additional testing tools and gathering evidence from target systems. Understanding how to implement data transfer capabilities enables development of comprehensive testing frameworks that can support complex testing scenarios while providing necessary data movement capabilities.

Protocol analysis and service interaction automation through Netcat integration enable testing of various network services and protocols while providing assessment of how services respond to different types of input and interaction patterns. Understanding how to implement protocol testing enables development of specialized testing tools that can assess service security while providing detailed evaluation of application-level security controls.

Curl Integration for Web Application Testing

Curl provides sophisticated HTTP and web service interaction capabilities that, when integrated with Bash scripting, enable comprehensive web application security testing while providing automated approaches for assessing web security controls and application vulnerabilities. Understanding how to leverage Curl effectively enables development of powerful web application testing frameworks that can assess security across diverse web technologies and implementations.

HTTP request automation and customization through Curl integration enable testing of web applications through various attack vectors while providing assessment of how applications respond to different types of malicious input and attack techniques. Understanding how to implement HTTP automation enables development of comprehensive web application testing tools that can assess security across multiple attack vectors while providing detailed evaluation of web security controls.

The implementation of effective Curl integration requires understanding how to construct appropriate HTTP requests, handle various response types, and implement error handling that enables testing tools to operate reliably across different web application environments while maintaining testing effectiveness and operational efficiency.

Authentication and session management testing through Curl integration enable assessment of web application authentication mechanisms while providing evaluation of how applications handle various authentication attack techniques and session manipulation attempts. Understanding how to implement authentication testing enables development of specialized web security assessment tools that can evaluate authentication security while providing comprehensive assessment of access control effectiveness.

Web service and API testing automation through Curl integration enable assessment of RESTful services, SOAP interfaces, and other web service implementations while providing evaluation of how APIs respond to various attack techniques and input validation bypass attempts. Understanding how to implement API testing enables development of comprehensive web service security assessment capabilities while maintaining efficient testing operation.

Content analysis and response parsing automation through Curl integration enable extraction of valuable information from web application responses while providing systematic analysis of application behavior and potential vulnerability indicators. Understanding how to implement response analysis enables development of intelligent web application testing tools that can identify potential security issues while providing detailed assessment of web application security posture.

Wget Integration for Data Acquisition

Wget provides powerful capabilities for automated data acquisition and web content retrieval that, when integrated with Bash scripting, enable comprehensive information gathering and reconnaissance activities while providing systematic approaches for collecting intelligence about target environments and applications.

Recursive web site downloading and analysis through Wget integration enable comprehensive assessment of web application structure and content while providing systematic collection of application files and resources for security analysis. Understanding how to implement recursive downloading enables development of thorough web application assessment tools that can gather complete application information while maintaining efficient operation and appropriate scope boundaries.

The implementation of effective Wget integration requires understanding how to manage download scope, handle various content types, and implement appropriate filtering mechanisms that enable testing tools to collect relevant information while avoiding excessive data collection that might impact testing efficiency or exceed appropriate testing boundaries.

Content filtering and selective acquisition through Wget integration enable focused collection of specific types of content while providing efficient gathering of security-relevant information without excessive data collection. Understanding how to implement selective acquisition enables development of efficient reconnaissance tools that can gather necessary intelligence while maintaining appropriate operational characteristics for professional security testing.

Mirror creation and offline analysis capabilities through Wget integration enable creation of local copies of web applications for detailed security analysis while providing comprehensive assessment capabilities that do not require continuous network access to target systems. Understanding how to implement mirror creation enables development of thorough web application analysis capabilities while providing flexible testing approaches that can accommodate various operational requirements.

Automated link analysis and discovery through Wget integration enable systematic identification of web application components and hidden content while providing comprehensive mapping of application structure and functionality. Understanding how to implement link analysis enables development of thorough reconnaissance tools that can discover application components while providing comprehensive assessment of web application attack surface.

Tool Chain Orchestration and Integration

The effective combination of Bash scripting with multiple networking tools requires sophisticated orchestration capabilities that can coordinate different tools while providing unified interfaces and comprehensive automation frameworks. Understanding how to implement tool chain orchestration enables development of professional-quality testing frameworks that leverage the strengths of multiple tools while providing efficient, reliable operation for complex security testing scenarios.

Workflow coordination and sequencing enable systematic execution of complex testing scenarios that combine multiple tools and techniques while providing appropriate error handling and recovery mechanisms for situations where individual components encounter problems. Understanding how to implement workflow coordination enables development of robust testing frameworks that can handle complex scenarios while maintaining reliable operation and providing comprehensive security assessment capabilities.

The implementation of effective workflow orchestration requires understanding how different tools interact with each other and how to manage dependencies, resource usage, and timing considerations that affect overall testing effectiveness while ensuring that combined tool usage provides enhanced capabilities compared to individual tool operation.

Data pipeline management and integration enable efficient flow of information between different tools while providing systematic processing and analysis of testing results across multiple tool outputs. Understanding how to implement data pipeline management enables development of comprehensive testing frameworks that can correlate information from multiple sources while providing unified analysis and reporting capabilities.

Error handling and fault tolerance across multiple tool chains enable testing frameworks to continue operating effectively even when individual tools encounter problems while providing appropriate recovery mechanisms and alternative approaches for maintaining testing effectiveness. Understanding how to implement fault tolerance enables development of reliable testing frameworks that can handle diverse operational conditions while maintaining comprehensive testing capabilities.

Performance optimization and resource management across integrated tool chains enable efficient operation of complex testing scenarios while managing system resource usage and maintaining appropriate timing characteristics for professional security testing activities. Understanding how to implement performance optimization enables development of scalable testing frameworks that can handle enterprise-level testing requirements while maintaining operational efficiency and effectiveness.

Conclusion

This chapter has established comprehensive offensive security automation capabilities that enable development of sophisticated penetration testing tools while maintaining strict adherence to professional, ethical, and legal standards for authorized security testing. From advanced payload development and social engineering automation to reverse shell implementation and network tool integration, you've developed skills that enable effective security assessment while demonstrating advanced automation techniques that provide immediate value for professional penetration testing activities.

The progression from individual offensive techniques to integrated attack frameworks demonstrates how fundamental scripting capabilities can be combined with security knowledge to create sophisticated testing tools that provide comprehensive security assessment capabilities. The techniques covered in this chapter—payload development, social engineering automation, reverse shell implementation, and network tool integration—represent core competencies that enable effective offensive security testing while maintaining appropriate professional standards and operational boundaries.

The offensive security frameworks developed throughout this chapter provide practical templates for creating comprehensive testing capabilities that can adapt to various engagement requirements while maintaining professional standards for reliability, stealth, and operational security. These frameworks demonstrate how individual attack techniques combine to create testing capabilities that provide thorough security assessment while maintaining appropriate safeguards for authorized testing activities.

The automation skills developed in this chapter enable systematic development and deployment of offensive security tools that would otherwise require substantial manual effort while providing more consistent and comprehensive testing results than ad-hoc manual approaches. More importantly, these automation capabilities enable security professionals to focus their expertise on analysis, strategy, and advanced testing techniques while delegating routine tool development and deployment tasks to reliable automated systems.

Moving forward, the offensive security automation capabilities established in this chapter provide the foundation for more advanced security testing projects including comprehensive red team automation, advanced persistent threat simulation, and integrated security assessment platforms. The patterns and practices demonstrated here—ethical development standards, professional operational security, comprehensive documentation, and appropriate scope management—will serve as templates for all future offensive security automation development while ensuring that your tools maintain the reliability and professionalism required for authorized security testing activities.

The investment you've made in understanding these offensive security automation techniques will pay dividends throughout your cybersecurity career as you encounter new challenges that require sophisticated testing capabilities while maintaining appropriate ethical and legal boundaries. With these capabilities firmly established, you're ready to explore more advanced automation topics that build upon this offensive foundation while addressing other critical areas of cybersecurity operations such as purple team automation, threat emulation frameworks, and comprehensive security assessment platforms that leverage these offensive capabilities in support of defensive improvement initiatives.

Important Legal and Ethical Notice: All techniques presented in this chapter are intended exclusively for authorized penetration testing, security research, and educational purposes conducted within appropriate legal frameworks with explicit permission from system owners. The use of these techniques against systems without proper authorization is illegal and unethical. Security professionals have a responsibility to use these capabilities only within appropriate professional, legal, and ethical boundaries while maintaining the highest standards of professional conduct and regulatory compliance.

Chapter 6: Secure Bash Scripting Practices

Security automation scripts occupy a unique position in cybersecurity infrastructure, serving as both defensive tools and potential attack vectors if not implemented with appropriate security considerations. The same capabilities that make Bash scripting powerful for security automation—system access, network communication, and administrative privileges—also create significant security risks when scripts contain vulnerabilities or are designed without adequate security controls. Understanding how to develop secure scripts while avoiding common security pitfalls is essential for creating automation tools that enhance rather than compromise overall security posture.

The history of cybersecurity is filled with examples of automation tools and scripts that became vectors for compromise due to inadequate security design, poor input validation, or insufficient access controls. These incidents demonstrate that security professionals must apply the same rigorous security principles to their automation tools that they would apply to any other system component. The development of secure scripts requires understanding not only how to implement intended functionality but also how to prevent unintended behaviors that could be exploited by attackers who gain access to script systems or who can influence script inputs.

This chapter explores comprehensive approaches to secure script development that address the full lifecycle of security automation from initial design and implementation through deployment, maintenance, and eventual retirement. Rather than simply listing security best practices, we examine the underlying principles that drive secure development while providing practical techniques for implementing robust security controls within script-based automation systems. The goal is to develop security-conscious scripting practices that become second nature, enabling creation of automation tools that enhance security rather than creating new vulnerabilities.

The progression through this chapter builds from fundamental security principles and common vulnerability patterns to advanced defensive techniques and real-world case studies that demonstrate both successful secure implementations and lessons learned from security failures. Each section emphasizes not only technical implementation details but also the security reasoning that drives design decisions, enabling development of security intuition that applies across diverse scripting scenarios and changing threat landscapes.

Avoiding Common Security Flaws in Scripts

Script security vulnerabilities often arise from common patterns and practices that seem innocuous during development but create exploitable conditions when scripts operate in production environments. Understanding these vulnerability patterns enables development of secure coding practices that prevent security issues before they occur while establishing defensive development habits that protect against both known attack techniques and novel exploitation methods.

Command Injection Prevention

Command injection represents one of the most severe security vulnerabilities in shell scripts, occurring when user input or external data is incorporated into command execution without proper validation and sanitization. The dynamic nature of shell scripting, which enables powerful automation capabilities, also creates numerous opportunities for command injection if input handling is not implemented securely from the outset.

Understanding command injection attack vectors requires recognizing how shell metacharacters and command separators can be used to modify intended command behavior while executing arbitrary additional commands. Common injection techniques leverage characters like semicolons, ampersands, pipe symbols, and command substitution operators that have special meaning in shell contexts and can alter script execution flow in unintended ways.

The fundamental principle for preventing command injection involves treating all external input as potentially malicious while implementing multiple layers of validation and sanitization that prevent injection attacks even when individual controls might be bypassed. This defense-in-depth approach ensures that command injection prevention remains effective even as attack techniques evolve, and new injection methods are discovered.

Input sanitization techniques for command injection prevention include whitelist validation that permits only known safe characters, blacklist filtering that removes dangerous metacharacters, and escape sequence handling that neutralizes special characters while preserving legitimate input values. Understanding how to implement comprehensive sanitization enables creation of scripts that can handle diverse input safely while maintaining functional effectiveness.

Parameterized command execution provides the most robust defense against command injection by separating command structure from data values while ensuring that user input cannot modify intended command behavior regardless of its content. Implementation of parameterized execution requires understanding how to construct commands that maintain clear separation between code and data while providing necessary functionality for automation tasks.

Privilege separation and least privilege principles minimize the potential impact of command injection vulnerabilities by ensuring that scripts operate with only the minimum privileges necessary for their intended functions. Understanding how to implement effective privilege controls enables creation of scripts that limit exposure even when other security controls might be bypassed or fail under attack conditions.

Path Traversal and File Access Vulnerabilities

Path traversal vulnerabilities enable attackers to access files and directories outside intended script scope by manipulating file path parameters to reference arbitrary filesystem locations. These vulnerabilities are particularly dangerous in security automation scripts that often require file system access for configuration management, log processing, and system monitoring activities.

Understanding path traversal attack techniques requires recognizing how relative path references, symbolic links, and special directory names can be manipulated to access sensitive files while bypassing intended access controls. Common attack vectors include directory traversal sequences like "../" that can navigate up directory hierarchies and symbolic link attacks that can redirect file access to arbitrary locations.

Absolute path validation provides fundamental protection against path traversal attacks by ensuring that all file access operations use fully qualified paths that cannot be manipulated through relative path injection. Implementation of absolute path validation requires understanding how to resolve and validate paths while preventing symbolic link and junction attacks that might bypass path restrictions.

Chroot environments and filesystem sandboxing provide additional layers of protection by restricting script file access to specific directory trees while preventing access to sensitive system areas even if path validation controls are bypassed. Understanding how to implement effective sandboxing enables creation of scripts that can access necessary files while maintaining strong isolation from critical system components.

File permission validation ensures that scripts respect existing filesystem access controls while preventing privilege escalation through file access operations. Understanding how to implement permission checking enables creation of scripts that operate safely within established security boundaries while avoiding unintended access to protected resources.

Canonical path resolution and validation prevent various bypass techniques that use complex path constructions to evade simple path filtering while ensuring that all file access operations are evaluated against consistent, normalized path representations. Understanding canonical path handling enables creation of robust file access controls that resist sophisticated bypass attempts.

Environment Variable and Configuration Security

Environment variables and configuration data represent significant attack surfaces in shell scripts because they provide mechanisms for external influence over script behavior while often receiving insufficient security consideration during development. Understanding how to secure configuration handling enables creation of scripts that can adapt to different environments while maintaining security boundaries.

Environment variable injection attacks exploit scripts that use environment variables without proper validation while enabling attackers to modify script behavior through manipulation of environment settings. Understanding injection risks requires recognizing how environment variables can influence script execution while implementing validation that prevents malicious manipulation of script behavior.

Configuration file security requires treating configuration data as potentially compromised while implementing validation and access controls that prevent configuration manipulation from leading to security vulnerabilities. Understanding configuration security enables creation of scripts that can use external configuration safely while maintaining security boundaries even when configuration sources might be compromised.

Default value security and fallback handling ensure that scripts behave securely even when expected configuration values are missing or invalid while preventing attacks that rely on forcing scripts to use insecure default configurations. Understanding secure defaults enables creation of scripts that maintain security posture even under adverse configuration conditions.

Configuration validation and type checking prevent configuration-based attacks by ensuring that all configuration values meet expected format and content requirements while rejecting potentially malicious configuration data before it can influence script behavior. Understanding configuration validation enables creation of robust scripts that handle configuration errors gracefully while maintaining security.

Encrypted configuration storage and secure configuration distribution protect sensitive configuration data while ensuring that configuration secrets cannot be easily accessed by unauthorized users or processes. Understanding configuration protection enables creation of scripts that can handle sensitive configuration data securely while maintaining operational effectiveness.

Race Condition and Timing Attack Prevention

Race conditions in scripts create security vulnerabilities when the timing of operations can be manipulated to create windows of opportunity for attack while enabling unauthorized access or privilege escalation. Understanding race condition vulnerabilities enables development of scripts that maintain security even under concurrent access and timing manipulation scenarios.

File creation and modification race conditions occur when scripts create temporary files or modify existing files without proper atomic operations while creating opportunities for attackers to manipulate file contents or substitute malicious files during processing windows. Understanding file operation security enables creation of scripts that handle file operations safely even under concurrent access conditions.

Atomic operation implementation ensures that critical script operations complete entirely or not at all while preventing partial state conditions that might be exploitable through timing manipulation. Understanding atomic operations enables creation of scripts that maintain consistent state even when interrupted or manipulated through timing attacks.

Temporary file security requires creating temporary files with appropriate permissions and in secure locations while ensuring that temporary files cannot be predicted or manipulated by attackers. Understanding temporary file handling enables creation of scripts that use temporary storage safely while avoiding common temporary file vulnerabilities.

Lock file implementation and process synchronization prevent multiple script instances from interfering with each other while ensuring that critical operations are protected against concurrent access that might create security vulnerabilities. Understanding synchronization techniques enables creation of scripts that coordinate safely with other processes while maintaining security boundaries.

Signal handling security ensures that scripts respond appropriately to system signals while preventing signal-based attacks that might interrupt critical operations or cause scripts to enter insecure states. Understanding signal security enables creation of robust scripts that handle system events securely while maintaining operational integrity.

Input Validation and Sandboxing Techniques

Robust input validation and effective sandboxing represent fundamental security controls that protect scripts against malicious input while limiting potential damage from successful attacks. Understanding how to implement comprehensive input validation and sandboxing enables creation of scripts that can handle untrusted input safely while maintaining necessary functionality for security automation tasks.

Comprehensive Input Validation Strategies

Effective input validation requires systematic approaches that examine all external input sources while implementing multiple validation layers that protect against diverse attack vectors. Understanding comprehensive validation strategies enables creation of scripts that can handle complex input requirements while maintaining strong security boundaries against malicious data.

Whitelist validation provides the strongest security approach by defining acceptable input values explicitly while rejecting anything that doesn't conform to expected patterns. Implementation of whitelist validation requires understanding how to define comprehensive acceptable value sets while ensuring that legitimate use cases are not inadvertently blocked by overly restrictive validation rules.

The development of effective whitelist validation requires careful analysis of legitimate input requirements while balancing security with usability to ensure that validation rules protect against attacks without creating excessive operational overhead or user friction. This systematic approach enables creation of validation systems that provide strong security while maintaining practical effectiveness.

Data type validation ensures that input values conform to expected data types while preventing type confusion attacks that rely on providing unexpected data types to bypass security controls. Understanding type validation enables creation of scripts that handle diverse input types safely while maintaining appropriate type safety throughout processing workflows.

Format validation verifies that input data conforms to expected structural patterns while preventing format string attacks and other techniques that rely on malformed input to exploit processing vulnerabilities. Understanding format validation enables creation of robust input processing that can handle complex data formats while maintaining security boundaries.

Length and boundary validation prevents buffer overflow and resource exhaustion attacks by ensuring that input data falls within acceptable size limits while protecting script resources from excessive consumption. Understanding boundary validation enables creation of scripts that can handle variable-size input safely while maintaining performance and stability characteristics.

Encoding and character set validation prevents encoding-based attacks that use character set manipulation to bypass security controls while ensuring that text processing operations handle character data safely across different encoding schemes. Understanding encoding validation enables creation of scripts that process international text safely while preventing encoding-based security vulnerabilities.

Advanced Sanitization Techniques

Input sanitization transforms potentially dangerous input into safe forms while preserving legitimate data values and maintaining functional effectiveness. Understanding advanced sanitization techniques enables creation of scripts that can process complex input safely while maintaining necessary functionality for automation tasks.

HTML and XML sanitization prevents markup injection attacks by removing or encoding dangerous markup elements while preserving legitimate content structure. Understanding markup sanitization enables creation of scripts that process web content safely while maintaining necessary markup processing capabilities for security automation tasks.

SQL injection prevention through parameterized queries and input sanitization protects database interactions from injection attacks while maintaining necessary database functionality for security automation. Understanding SQL sanitization enables creation of scripts that interact with databases safely while preventing unauthorized database access or manipulation.

Regular expression sanitization and validation provide flexible pattern-matching capabilities for input validation while preventing regular expression denial of service attacks and injection techniques that use malicious patterns to exploit regex processing. Understanding regex security enables creation of flexible validation systems that handle complex patterns safely.

Shell command sanitization prevents command injection while enabling scripts to construct system commands safely when parameterized execution is not practical. Understanding command sanitization enables creation of scripts that can build system commands dynamically while maintaining protection against injection attacks.

Unicode normalization and security considerations prevent attacks that use Unicode character variations to bypass validation while ensuring that text processing handles international characters consistently and securely. Understanding Unicode security enables creation of scripts that process international text safely while preventing Unicode-based bypass techniques.

Containerization and Isolation Techniques

Containerization and process isolation provide additional security layers that limit script capabilities while containing potential damage from successful attacks. Understanding isolation techniques enables creation of scripts that operate within well-defined security boundaries while maintaining necessary functionality for automation tasks.

Container-based sandboxing provides comprehensive isolation by running scripts within containerized environments that limit access to host system resources while providing controlled access to necessary services and data. Understanding container security enables creation of script deployment strategies that provide strong isolation while maintaining operational effectiveness.

The implementation of effective container-based sandboxing requires understanding how to configure container security policies, resource limits, and network access controls that provide appropriate isolation while enabling scripts to access necessary resources for their intended functions. This systematic approach enables creation of secure deployment environments that protect against script-based attacks.

Chroot environment implementation provides filesystem isolation that restricts script access to specific directory trees while preventing access to sensitive system areas. Understanding chroot security enables creation of script environments that provide necessary file access while maintaining strong filesystem isolation boundaries.

Namespace isolation and resource limiting prevent scripts from interfering with other system processes while limiting resource consumption that might enable denial of service attacks. Understanding namespace security enables creation of script environments that provide appropriate isolation while maintaining system stability and performance.

User account isolation and privilege dropping ensure that scripts operate with minimum necessary privileges while preventing privilege escalation attacks that might leverage script vulnerabilities to gain elevated system access. Understanding privilege management enables creation of scripts that operate securely within established security boundaries.

Network segmentation and firewall controls limit script network access to necessary services while preventing network-based attacks that might leverage script functionality to access internal systems or exfiltrate data. Understanding network isolation enables creation of script environments that provide necessary connectivity while maintaining network security boundaries.

Runtime Security Monitoring

Runtime security monitoring provides ongoing protection against attacks that might bypass static security controls while enabling detection and response to security events during script execution.

Understanding runtime monitoring enables creation of scripts that provide security visibility while maintaining operational effectiveness.

System call monitoring and anomaly detection identify unusual script behavior that might indicate compromise or attack while providing early warning of security events that require investigation or response. Understanding system call monitoring enables creation of scripts that provide security telemetry while maintaining performance characteristics.

Resource usage monitoring prevents denial of service attacks and resource exhaustion while ensuring that scripts operate within acceptable resource boundaries for their environments. Understanding resource monitoring enables creation of scripts that provide performance visibility while preventing resource-based attacks.

Network activity monitoring detects unusual communication patterns that might indicate compromise or misuse while providing visibility into script network behavior for security assessment and incident response. Understanding network monitoring enables creation of scripts that provide network security telemetry while maintaining necessary connectivity.

File access monitoring tracks script file operations while detecting unauthorized access attempts or suspicious file manipulation that might indicate security issues. Understanding file monitoring enables creation of scripts that provide filesystem security visibility while maintaining necessary file access capabilities.

Log analysis and security event correlation enable detection of complex attack patterns that span multiple activities while providing comprehensive security assessment of script behavior over time. Understanding security event analysis enables creation of monitoring systems that provide actionable security intelligence while maintaining operational efficiency.

Logging, Error Handling, and Fail-Safes

Comprehensive logging, robust error handling, and reliable fail-safe mechanisms represent critical components of secure script design that provide both operational visibility and security protection. Understanding how to implement these defensive mechanisms enables creation of scripts that provide detailed audit trails while handling unexpected conditions securely and maintaining operational integrity even under attack conditions.

Security-Focused Logging Implementation

Security-focused logging provides essential visibility into script operation while creating audit trails that support incident investigation and compliance requirements. Understanding how to implement comprehensive security logging enables creation of scripts that provide actionable security intelligence while maintaining appropriate log security and integrity.

Comprehensive audit logging captures all security-relevant script activities while providing detailed records of user actions, system interactions, and security decisions that support investigation and compliance activities. Understanding audit logging enables creation of scripts that provide complete operational visibility while maintaining appropriate detail levels for security assessment.

The implementation of effective audit logging requires understanding which activities have security significance and how to capture appropriate detail levels that support investigation while avoiding excessive logging that might impact performance or create storage challenges. This systematic approach enables creation of logging systems that provide valuable security intelligence while maintaining operational efficiency.

Sensitive data protection in logs prevents disclosure of confidential information while maintaining necessary audit functionality for security and compliance purposes. Understanding log data protection enables creation of logging systems that provide security visibility while protecting sensitive information from unauthorized disclosure through log access.

Log integrity protection prevents log tampering and manipulation while ensuring that audit records maintain evidential value for investigation and compliance purposes. Understanding log protection enables creation of logging systems that provide reliable audit trails while protecting against attempts to conceal malicious activities through log modification.

Structured logging and standardization enable efficient log analysis and correlation while providing consistent log formats that support automated analysis and integration with security information and event management systems. Understanding structured logging enables creation of logging systems that provide actionable intelligence while supporting automated security analysis.

Remote logging and centralized collection provide protection against local log tampering while ensuring that security events are preserved even if local systems are compromised. Understanding remote logging enables creation of distributed logging systems that provide comprehensive security visibility while maintaining log integrity across diverse deployment environments.

Robust Error Handling and Recovery

Robust error handling ensures that scripts respond appropriately to unexpected conditions while maintaining security boundaries and preventing error conditions from creating security vulnerabilities. Understanding comprehensive error handling enables creation of scripts that handle failures gracefully while maintaining security posture even under adverse conditions.

Error classification and response strategies enable scripts to respond appropriately to different types of errors while implementing graduated response mechanisms that match response intensity to error severity. Understanding error classification enables creation of scripts that handle diverse failure modes effectively while maintaining appropriate security and operational responses.

The implementation of effective error handling requires understanding how different types of errors might impact script security and functionality while designing response mechanisms that preserve security boundaries while enabling appropriate recovery actions. This systematic approach enables creation of resilient scripts that maintain security even when encountering unexpected conditions.

Secure error reporting prevents information disclosure through error messages while providing sufficient detail for troubleshooting and investigation purposes. Understanding secure error reporting enables creation of scripts that provide useful diagnostic information while preventing attackers from gaining intelligence about system configuration or security controls through error message analysis.

Graceful degradation and fallback mechanisms enable scripts to continue operating with reduced functionality when optimal operation is not possible while maintaining security boundaries and preventing degraded operation from creating security vulnerabilities. Understanding graceful degradation enables creation of resilient scripts that maintain essential functions even under adverse conditions.

Recovery and rollback capabilities enable scripts to return to known good states when errors occur while preventing partial operations from leaving systems in inconsistent or vulnerable states. Understanding recovery mechanisms enables creation of scripts that can handle failures safely while maintaining system integrity and security posture.

Exception handling security prevents exception-based attacks that rely on triggering error conditions to bypass security controls while ensuring that error handling code itself doesn't introduce security vulnerabilities. Understanding exception security enables creation of robust error handling that maintains security boundaries even when processing unexpected conditions.

Fail-Safe Design Principles

Fail-safe design ensures that scripts default to secure states when encountering unexpected conditions while preventing failures from creating security vulnerabilities or operational hazards. Understanding fail-safe principles enables creation of scripts that maintain security even when normal operation is compromised.

Default-deny security policies ensure that scripts deny access by default while requiring explicit authorization for sensitive operations. Understanding default-deny principles enables creation of scripts that maintain strong security boundaries while preventing unauthorized access even when access control logic encounters unexpected conditions.

The implementation of effective fail-safe mechanisms requires understanding how scripts might fail and designing default behaviors that preserve security boundaries while enabling appropriate recovery actions when normal operation resumes. This systematic approach enables creation of scripts that maintain security even during failure conditions.

Safe failure modes prevent catastrophic failures from creating security vulnerabilities while ensuring that script failures don't compromise overall system security or enable unauthorized access. Understanding safe failure design enables creation of scripts that handle failures responsibly while maintaining appropriate security and operational boundaries.

Emergency shutdown and containment mechanisms enable rapid response to security incidents while preventing compromised scripts from causing additional damage or enabling further compromise. Understanding emergency response mechanisms enables creation of scripts that support incident response while maintaining appropriate containment and damage limitation capabilities.

Health check and monitoring integration enable early detection of script problems while providing automated response capabilities that can prevent minor issues from escalating into significant security incidents. Understanding health monitoring enables creation of scripts that provide operational visibility while supporting proactive problem resolution.

Backup and recovery integration ensures that critical script operations can be recovered from failures while maintaining data integrity and security boundaries throughout recovery processes. Understanding backup integration enables creation of scripts that provide operational resilience while maintaining security and compliance requirements.

Performance and Resource Management

Performance optimization and resource management prevent denial of service vulnerabilities while ensuring that scripts operate efficiently within available system resources. Understanding performance security enables creation of scripts that provide necessary functionality while protecting against resource-based attacks and operational disruptions.

Resource limit enforcement prevents resource exhaustion attacks while ensuring that scripts operate within acceptable bounds for their deployment environments. Understanding resource management enables creation of scripts that provide necessary functionality while protecting system stability and performance for other processes and users.

Memory management and leak prevention protect against memory exhaustion attacks while ensuring that scripts maintain stable memory usage patterns throughout their operational lifecycle. Understanding memory security enables creation of scripts that handle memory efficiently while preventing memory-based denial of service conditions.

CPU utilization control prevents processor exhaustion attacks while ensuring that scripts provide necessary functionality without monopolizing system computational resources. Understanding CPU management enables creation of scripts that balance functionality with resource responsibility while maintaining system responsiveness for other processes.

Network bandwidth management prevents network-based denial of service while ensuring that scripts can perform necessary network operations without overwhelming network infrastructure. Understanding bandwidth management enables creation of scripts that use network resources responsibly while maintaining necessary connectivity for automation tasks.

Storage space management prevents disk exhaustion attacks while ensuring that scripts can handle necessary data storage requirements without consuming excessive filesystem resources. Understanding storage management enables creation of scripts that handle data efficiently while protecting filesystem availability for other system functions.

Real-World Examples of Exploited Scripts

Understanding how security vulnerabilities in scripts have been exploited in real-world scenarios provides essential lessons for secure script development while demonstrating the practical impact of security flaws and the importance of implementing comprehensive security controls. Analysis of actual exploitation cases enables development of security intuition that helps identify potential vulnerabilities before they can be exploited.

Case Study Analysis of Script Vulnerabilities

Real-world script vulnerabilities provide concrete examples of how theoretical security principles apply in practice while demonstrating the progression from initial vulnerability discovery through exploitation and impact assessment. Understanding vulnerability case studies enables recognition of similar patterns in new development while informing security design decisions that prevent recurring vulnerability types.

Command injection exploitation cases demonstrate how inadequate input validation can lead to arbitrary command execution while showing the progression from initial input manipulation through privilege escalation and system compromise. Understanding command injection cases enables recognition of vulnerable patterns while informing development of robust input validation that prevents similar attacks.

Analysis of significant command injection incidents reveals common development practices that create vulnerabilities while demonstrating how seemingly minor input validation gaps can lead to complete system compromise. These cases show the importance of comprehensive input validation and parameterized command execution for preventing injection attacks while illustrating the potential impact of inadequate security controls.

Path traversal exploitation examples show how file access vulnerabilities can lead to unauthorized access to sensitive files while demonstrating techniques that attackers use to bypass simple path validation. Understanding path traversal cases enables development of robust file access controls that prevent directory traversal and symbolic link attacks while maintaining necessary filesystem functionality.

Configuration manipulation attacks demonstrate how inadequate configuration security can enable attackers to modify script behavior while showing the progression from configuration access through privilege escalation and persistence establishment. Understanding configuration attacks enables development of secure configuration handling that protects against manipulation while maintaining necessary flexibility for operational requirements.

Race condition exploitation cases show how timing vulnerabilities can be leveraged for privilege escalation while demonstrating the sophisticated techniques that attackers use to exploit timing windows in script operations. Understanding race condition attacks enables development of atomic operations and proper synchronization that prevent timing-based vulnerabilities while maintaining operational efficiency.

Vulnerability Pattern Recognition

Identifying common vulnerability patterns enables proactive security design that prevents entire classes of security issues while developing security intuition that applies across diverse scripting scenarios. Understanding vulnerability patterns enables systematic security assessment of scripts while informing development practices that prevent predictable security issues.

Input validation bypass patterns demonstrate how attackers identify and exploit gaps in validation logic while showing the iterative process that attackers use to test validation boundaries and discover bypasses. Understanding bypass patterns enables development of comprehensive validation that resists systematic testing while maintaining appropriate functional flexibility.

Privilege escalation patterns show how initial script access can be leveraged to gain elevated system privileges while demonstrating the common techniques that attackers use to expand their access from script compromise. Understanding escalation patterns enables development of privilege isolation and least privilege implementations that limit the impact of script compromise while maintaining necessary functionality.

Data exfiltration patterns demonstrate how compromised scripts can be used to access and transmit sensitive information while showing the techniques that attackers use to locate valuable data and establish covert communication channels. Understanding exfiltration patterns enables development of data protection and network isolation controls that prevent unauthorized data access while maintaining necessary operational capabilities.

Persistence establishment patterns show how attackers use compromised scripts to maintain long-term access while demonstrating the techniques used to survive system restarts and security updates. Understanding persistence patterns enables development of script isolation and monitoring capabilities that detect unauthorized persistence while maintaining legitimate script functionality.

Lateral movement patterns demonstrate how script compromise can be used to access additional systems while showing the progression from initial compromise through network reconnaissance and additional system access. Understanding lateral movement patterns enables development of network segmentation and access controls that limit the scope of script compromise while maintaining necessary connectivity.

Lessons Learned and Best Practices

Analysis of real-world exploitation cases provides concrete lessons that inform secure development practices while demonstrating the practical value of specific security controls in preventing actual attacks. Understanding lessons learned enables development of security practices that address real-world threats while balancing security with operational requirements.

Defense-in-depth effectiveness is demonstrated through cases where multiple security controls prevented complete compromise even when individual controls were bypassed while showing the value of layered security approaches that provide multiple failure points for attackers. Understanding defense-in-depth successes enables development of comprehensive security architectures that resist sophisticated attacks.

Early detection and response successes show how monitoring and alerting systems can identify script compromise in progress while demonstrating the importance of security visibility and incident response capabilities for limiting attack impact. Understanding detection successes enables development of monitoring systems that provide actionable security intelligence while supporting rapid incident response.

Secure development lifecycle benefits are demonstrated through cases where security considerations during development prevented vulnerabilities that would have been exploitable in production while showing the cost-effectiveness of early security investment compared to post-deployment remediation. Understanding development lifecycle successes enables integration of security considerations throughout script development while maintaining development efficiency.

Security training and awareness impacts are shown through cases where developer security knowledge prevented common vulnerabilities while demonstrating the value of security education for development teams. Understanding training impacts enables development of security-conscious development practices that become standard procedure while maintaining development productivity and code quality.

Incident response and recovery effectiveness is demonstrated through cases where well-planned response procedures limited attack impact while showing the importance of preparation and practice for handling script compromise. Understanding response effectiveness enables development of incident response capabilities that support rapid containment while maintaining operational continuity during security events.

Preventive Measures and Mitigation Strategies

Understanding how real-world script vulnerabilities could have been prevented enables development of proactive security measures that address root causes while implementing systematic approaches to vulnerability prevention. Analysis of prevention opportunities enables development of security practices that eliminate entire vulnerability classes rather than addressing individual issues reactively.

Secure coding standard implementation demonstrates how consistent application of security principles can prevent common vulnerabilities while showing the practical value of established security guidelines for development teams. Understanding coding standards enables development of security practices that become routine while maintaining development efficiency and code quality.

Security testing and validation integration shows how systematic security testing can identify vulnerabilities before deployment while demonstrating the cost-effectiveness of early vulnerability detection compared to post-deployment incident response. Understanding testing integration enables development of security validation processes that identify issues early while maintaining development velocity and deployment schedules.

Security architecture and design review processes demonstrate how early security analysis can identify design vulnerabilities that would be difficult to address after implementation while showing the value of security expertise during design phases. Understanding architecture review enables integration of security considerations into design processes while maintaining development efficiency and architectural quality.

Continuous security monitoring and improvement practices show how ongoing security assessment can identify emerging threats and adaptation requirements while demonstrating the value of security as an ongoing process rather than a one-time activity. Understanding continuous improvement enables development of security practices that adapt to changing threats while maintaining operational effectiveness and security posture.

Conclusion

This chapter has established comprehensive secure scripting practices that enable development of robust, secure automation tools while understanding and preventing the security vulnerabilities that can turn security scripts into attack vectors. From fundamental vulnerability prevention and comprehensive input validation to robust error handling and real-world case study analysis, you've developed security-conscious development practices that ensure your automation tools enhance rather than compromise security posture.

The progression from basic security principles to advanced defensive techniques and real-world vulnerability analysis demonstrates how security must be integrated throughout the script development lifecycle rather than treated as an afterthought. The techniques covered in this chapter—secure input handling, comprehensive validation, defensive programming practices, and systematic vulnerability prevention—represent core competencies that distinguish professional security automation from ad-hoc scripting approaches that may introduce security risks.

The defensive frameworks and security practices developed throughout this chapter provide practical templates for creating secure automation that can handle untrusted input safely while maintaining strong security boundaries even under attack conditions. These frameworks demonstrate how individual security controls combine to create defense-in-depth protection that remains effective even when individual controls might be bypassed or fail under sophisticated attack.

The security skills developed in this chapter enable systematic identification and prevention of script vulnerabilities while implementing comprehensive security controls that protect against both known attack techniques and novel exploitation methods. More importantly, these security practices enable development of security intuition that helps identify potential vulnerabilities during design and implementation phases when they can be addressed efficiently and effectively.

Moving forward, the secure scripting practices established in this chapter provide the foundation for all future automation development while ensuring that security considerations are integrated naturally into development processes. The patterns and practices demonstrated here—comprehensive input validation, defense-in-depth design, robust error handling, and systematic vulnerability analysis—will serve as templates for maintaining security throughout increasingly complex automation projects while ensuring that your tools meet the reliability and security standards required for cybersecurity operations.

The investment you've made in understanding secure scripting practices will pay dividends throughout your cybersecurity career as you develop automation tools that handle sensitive data, operate in hostile environments, and provide critical security functions. With these security-conscious development practices firmly established, you can create automation tools that not only provide necessary functionality but also maintain the security integrity essential for effective cybersecurity operations. The security principles and defensive techniques covered in this chapter will continue to guide your development efforts while adapting to new threats and evolving security requirements throughout your professional career.

Chapter 7: Scheduling and Monitoring with Cron and Bash

In the realm of cybersecurity and system administration, automation stands as one of the most powerful tools at your disposal. The ability to schedule and monitor security tasks without constant human intervention not only improves efficiency but also ensures that critical security measures are consistently applied across your infrastructure. This chapter explores the integration of cron, Unix's time-based job scheduler, with Bash scripting to create robust, automated security solutions that can run around the clock, protecting your systems even when you're not actively monitoring them.

The marriage of cron and Bash scripting creates a formidable combination for cybersecurity professionals. While cron provides the scheduling backbone that ensures tasks run at precise intervals, Bash scripts deliver the intelligence and flexibility needed to perform complex security operations. Together, they enable you to build comprehensive security automation frameworks that can handle everything from routine log analysis to emergency response procedures.

Understanding Cron Fundamentals

Cron operates as a daemon process that runs continuously in the background of Unix-like operating systems, checking every minute for scheduled tasks that need execution. The system relies on crontab files, which contain lists of commands scheduled to run at specific times. Each user can have their own crontab, while the system maintains a global crontab for system-wide tasks. Understanding cron's architecture is crucial for implementing effective security automation, as it forms the foundation upon which all scheduled security tasks will operate.

The cron time format consists of five fields representing minute, hour, day of month, month, and day of week. Each field can contain specific values, ranges, lists, or special characters that provide tremendous flexibility in scheduling. For instance, an asterisk (*) means "any value," while a slash (/) indicates step values. This syntax allows you to create schedules ranging from every minute to specific combinations like "every Tuesday at 3:30 AM during the first week of each quarter."

Cron Syntax and Time Specifications

Mastering cron syntax is essential for creating precise scheduling patterns that align with your security requirements. The five-field format follows the pattern: minute (0-59), hour (0-23), day of month (1-31), month (1-12), and day of week (0-7, where both 0 and 7 represent Sunday). Special characters extend this basic syntax significantly. The comma allows multiple values (1,15 means first and fifteenth), the hyphen creates ranges (1-5 means Monday through Friday), and the slash creates step values (*/15 means every 15 units).

Advanced cron implementations support additional special strings that simplify common scheduling patterns. @yearly or @annually runs once per year, @monthly executes monthly, @weekly runs weekly, @daily or @midnight executes daily at midnight, @hourly runs every hour, and @reboot executes at system startup. These shortcuts prove particularly useful for security tasks that follow standard intervals, such as weekly vulnerability scans or daily log rotations.

Security Considerations for Cron Usage

When implementing cron for security automation, several security considerations demand attention. Cron jobs run with the privileges of the user who owns the crontab, making proper user account management critical. Security scripts should ideally run under dedicated service accounts with minimal necessary privileges, following the principle of least privilege. This approach limits potential damage if a scheduled script becomes compromised or behaves unexpectedly.

Environment variables in cron jobs differ significantly from interactive shell sessions, which can cause scripts to fail unexpectedly. Cron provides a minimal environment, typically including only HOME, LOGNAME, PATH, and SHELL variables. Security scripts must explicitly set required environment variables or use absolute paths for all external commands. Additionally, cron job output handling requires careful consideration, as uncaptured output gets emailed to the job owner, potentially exposing sensitive information.

Automating Scripts Using Cron

The integration of Bash scripts with cron scheduling creates powerful automation capabilities for cybersecurity tasks. Effective automation requires careful script design that accounts for cron's unique execution environment and implements proper error handling, logging, and notification mechanisms. Scripts running under cron must be completely autonomous, handling all potential error conditions gracefully without requiring human intervention.

When designing scripts for cron execution, consider the script's runtime environment carefully. Unlike interactive shells, cron jobs execute in a minimal environment without access to aliases, functions, or custom environment variables defined in shell configuration files. This limitation necessitates using absolute paths for all external commands and explicitly setting any required environment variables within the script itself.

Designing Cron-Compatible Scripts

Creating scripts that work reliably under cron requires adherence to several best practices that ensure consistent execution regardless of the scheduling context. Scripts should begin with a proper shebang line (#!/bin/bash) and set the PATH variable explicitly to include all directories containing required executables. Error handling becomes particularly critical in automated environments, as scripts must gracefully handle unexpected conditions without human intervention.

Lock file mechanisms prevent multiple instances of the same script from running simultaneously, which could cause resource conflicts or data corruption. A typical implementation creates a lock file at script startup and removes it upon completion, with logic to check for existing lock files before proceeding. This approach proves essential for long-running security scans or analysis tasks that might overlap if system performance is degraded.

```
#!/bin/bash
LOCKFILE="/var/run/security_scan.lock"
LOGFILE="/var/log/security/automated_scan.log"
# Function to cleanup lock file on exit
cleanup() {
rm -f "$LOCKFILE"
exit $1
}
# Set trap to cleanup on various exit conditions
trap 'cleanup $?' INT TERM EXIT
# Check for existing lock file
if [ -f "$LOCKFILE" ]; then
echo "$(date): Script already running, exiting" >> "$LOGFILE"
exit 1
fi
# Create lock file
echo $$ > "$LOCKFILE"
# Main script logic here
echo "$(date): Starting automated security scan" >> "$LOGFILE"
```

Managing Script Dependencies and Paths

Cron's minimal environment often causes scripts to fail when they depend on specific PATH settings or environment variables available in interactive sessions. Establishing a robust approach to dependency management ensures scripts execute reliably regardless of the cron environment. This involves explicitly setting PATH variables, using absolute paths for external commands, and implementing checks for required dependencies before script execution begins.

Creating a standard environment setup function that can be sourced by all cron scripts provides consistency across your automation framework. This function should set common paths, establish logging configurations, and verify the availability of required tools and services. Additionally, implementing version checks for critical dependencies helps identify potential issues before they cause script failures in production environments.

Creating Time-Based Security Tasks

Time-based security tasks form the backbone of proactive cybersecurity measures, enabling organizations to maintain consistent security postures through automated monitoring, scanning, and maintenance activities. These tasks range from simple log rotation and cleanup procedures to complex vulnerability assessments and threat hunting operations. The key to successful time-based security automation lies in understanding the appropriate frequency for different types of security activities and designing scripts that can adapt to changing conditions.

Different security tasks require different scheduling approaches based on their impact on system resources, the urgency of their output, and their relationship to other security processes. High-frequency tasks like log monitoring might run every few minutes, while comprehensive vulnerability scans might execute weekly or monthly. Understanding these timing relationships helps create efficient automation schedules that maximize security coverage while minimizing system impact.

Daily Security Maintenance Tasks

Daily security maintenance encompasses routine activities that ensure systems remain secure and properly configured. These tasks typically include log analysis, security update checks, certificate expiration monitoring, and basic system health verification. Daily tasks should focus on quick, efficient operations that provide immediate security value without consuming excessive system resources during business hours.

Log analysis automation represents one of the most valuable daily security tasks. Scripts can parse various log files, identify suspicious patterns, extract relevant security events, and generate summarized reports for security teams. Effective log analysis automation requires understanding log formats, implementing efficient parsing techniques, and creating meaningful alerts that don't overwhelm security personnel with false positives.

```
#!/bin/bash
# Daily security log analysis script
LOG_DIR="/var/log"
REPORT_DIR="/var/log/security/daily_reports"
DATE=$(date +%Y%m%d)
REPORT_FILE="$REPORT_DIR/security_report_$DATE.txt"
# Create report directory if it doesn't exist
mkdir -p "$REPORT_DIR"
# Analyze auth logs for failed login attempts
echo "=== Failed Login Analysis ===" > "$REPORT_FILE"
grep "Failed password" "$LOG_DIR/auth.log" | awk '{print $1, $2, $3, $9, $11}' | sort | uniq -c | sort -nr >> "$REPORT_FILE"
# Check for privilege escalation attempts
echo -e "\n=== Privilege Escalation Attempts ===" >> "$REPORT_FILE"
grep -E "(sudo|su).*COMMAND" "$LOG_DIR/auth.log" | tail -20 >> "$REPORT_FILE"
# Analyze network connections
echo -e "\n=== Unusual Network Connections ===" >> "$REPORT_FILE"
netstat -an | grep ESTABLISHED | awk '{print $5}' | cut -d: -f1 | sort | uniq -c | sort -nr | head -10 >> "$REPORT_FILE"
```

Weekly and Monthly Security Assessments

Weekly and monthly security assessments involve more comprehensive evaluations that can consume significant system resources and require longer execution times. These tasks might include full system vulnerability scans, comprehensive log analysis, security policy compliance checks, and detailed system configuration audits. The extended timeframes allow for thorough analysis while ensuring these resource-intensive operations don't interfere with daily business activities.

Vulnerability scanning automation requires careful scheduling to balance thoroughness with system availability. Weekly scans might focus on external-facing services and critical systems, while monthly scans could perform comprehensive internal network assessments. Implementing intelligent scheduling that considers system load, business hours, and maintenance windows ensures these critical security activities don't negatively impact productivity.

Event-Driven Security Responses

Beyond time-based scheduling, modern security automation increasingly relies on event-driven responses that trigger based on specific conditions or thresholds. These responsive automation systems monitor various indicators and automatically execute appropriate countermeasures when threats are detected. Combining time-based monitoring with event-driven responses creates comprehensive security automation that addresses both proactive and reactive security needs.

Implementing event-driven security responses requires robust monitoring capabilities that can detect relevant security events in real-time. This might involve monitoring log files for specific patterns, checking system metrics for anomalous behavior, or integrating with external threat intelligence feeds. The automation framework must be capable of rapid response while maintaining appropriate safeguards to prevent false positive responses that could disrupt normal operations.

Logging Cron Activity and Securing Scheduled Jobs

Comprehensive logging of cron activities provides essential visibility into automated security processes, enabling administrators to verify successful execution, diagnose failures, and maintain audit trails for compliance purposes. Effective cron logging goes beyond simply capturing script output; it includes detailed execution tracking, performance metrics, error analysis, and security event correlation. This logging framework becomes particularly critical in security automation, where failed or compromised automated tasks could leave systems vulnerable.

Cron itself provides basic logging capabilities through the system logger, typically writing to /var/log/cron or similar locations depending on the system configuration. However, this basic logging often proves insufficient for comprehensive security automation monitoring. Enhanced logging strategies involve custom logging within scripts, centralized log management, and integration with security information and event management (SIEM) systems.

Implementing Comprehensive Cron Logging

Creating a robust logging framework for cron-based security automation requires designing logging strategies that capture all relevant information while remaining manageable and performant. Effective logging includes timestamped entries, execution status information, performance metrics, error details, and security-relevant events. This comprehensive approach enables both operational monitoring and security analysis of automated processes.

Structured logging approaches using formats like JSON or key-value pairs facilitate automated log analysis and integration with log management platforms. Scripts should implement consistent logging standards that include common fields such as timestamp, script name, execution ID, user context, and severity level. This standardization enables efficient log aggregation, searching, and alerting across the entire automation framework.

```
#!/bin/bash
# Enhanced logging function for security scripts
SCRIPT_NAME=$(basename "$0")
LOG_FILE="/var/log/security/cron_automation.log"
EXECUTION_ID=$(date +%s)_$$
log_message() {
local level="$1"
local message="$2"
local timestamp=$(date '+%Y-%m-%d %H:%M:%S')
# JSON structured logging
echo
"{\"timestamp\":\"$timestamp\",\"script\":\"$SCRIPT_NAME\",\"execution_id\":\"
$EXECUTION_ID\",\"level\":\"$level\",\"message\":\"$message\"}" >>
"$LOG_FILE"
# Also log to syslog for centralized collection
logger -t "security_automation" -p local0.$level
"$SCRIPT_NAME[$EXECUTION_ID]: $message"
}
# Usage examples
log_message "info" "Script execution started"
log_message "warning" "Unusual network traffic detected"
log_message "error" "Failed to connect to vulnerability database"
```

Securing Cron Jobs and Preventing Abuse

Securing scheduled jobs involves multiple layers of protection that address both accidental misconfiguration and malicious exploitation. Cron jobs often run with elevated privileges and access sensitive system resources, making them attractive targets for attackers seeking persistence or privilege escalation. Implementing robust security measures around cron jobs protects both the automation framework and the broader system infrastructure.

Access control for cron jobs begins with proper file permissions and ownership. Crontab files should be readable only by their owners and the cron daemon, preventing unauthorized users from viewing or modifying scheduled tasks. Additionally, implementing allow and deny lists through /etc/cron.allow and /etc/cron.deny files restrict which users can create cron jobs, limiting potential attack vectors.

Monitoring and Alerting for Cron Failures

Automated monitoring of cron job execution status ensures that critical security tasks complete successfully and alerts administrators to potential issues before they impact security posture. Effective monitoring encompasses both successful execution verification and failure detection, with appropriate escalation procedures for different types of failures. This monitoring framework should integrate with existing alerting systems and provide sufficient detail for rapid problem resolution.

Implementing intelligent alerting that distinguishes between different types of failures prevents alert fatigue while ensuring critical issues receive immediate attention. Transient network failures might warrant different responses than script logic errors or security policy violations. The monitoring system should track execution patterns, identify trends that might indicate systemic issues, and provide predictive insights that enable proactive maintenance.

Setting Up Watchdogs and Health Checks

Watchdog systems and health checks provide continuous monitoring capabilities that ensure security automation remains operational and effective. These systems monitor not only the execution of scheduled tasks but also the overall health of the automation infrastructure, including resource availability, service dependencies, and security policy compliance. Implementing comprehensive watchdog systems creates self-healing automation frameworks that can detect and respond to various failure conditions automatically.

Effective watchdog implementations operate at multiple levels, from individual script monitoring to system-wide health assessment. Script-level watchdogs verify that automated security tasks complete within expected timeframes and produce expected outputs. System-level watchdogs monitor resource utilization, service availability, and overall system health. Integration between these levels creates comprehensive monitoring that can identify and respond to issues before they impact security operations.

Implementing Process Monitoring

Process monitoring for security automation involves tracking the lifecycle of scheduled tasks, verifying their resource consumption stays within acceptable bounds, and ensuring they complete within expected timeframes. This monitoring extends beyond simple success or failure detection to include performance analysis, resource utilization tracking, and behavioral anomaly detection. Such comprehensive monitoring enables early identification of issues that might not immediately cause failures but could indicate underlying problems.

Automated process monitoring systems should implement configurable thresholds for various metrics including execution time, memory usage, CPU consumption, and network activity. When processes exceed these thresholds, the monitoring system can trigger appropriate responses ranging from simple alerts to automatic process termination and restart procedures. This approach prevents runaway processes from impacting system stability while maintaining visibility into automation performance.

```
#!/bin/bash
# Process monitoring watchdog for security automation
MONITOR_DIR="/var/run/security_monitors"
ALERT_THRESHOLD_CPU=80 # CPU percentage
ALERT_THRESHOLD_MEM=75 # Memory percentage
```

```
ALERT_THRESHOLD_TIME=3600 # Maximum execution time in seconds
monitor_process() {
local process_name="$1"
local pid_file="$MONITOR_DIR/${process_name}.pid"
if [ ! -f "$pid_file" ]; then
log_message "warning" "PID file not found for $process_name"
return 1
fi
local pid=$(cat "$pid_file")
# Check if process is still running
if ! kill -0 "$pid" 2>/dev/null; then
log_message "error" "Process $process_name (PID: $pid) is no longer running"
rm -f "$pid_file"
return 1
fi
# Get process statistics
local stats=$(ps -p "$pid" -o pid,ppid,pcpu,pmem,etime,comm—no-headers)
local cpu_usage=$(echo "$stats" | awk '{print $3}' | cut -d. -f1)
local mem_usage=$(echo "$stats" | awk '{print $4}' | cut -d. -f1)
local runtime=$(echo "$stats" | awk '{print $5}')
# Convert runtime to seconds for comparison
local runtime_seconds=$(convert_time_to_seconds "$runtime")
# Check thresholds and alert if necessary
if [ "$cpu_usage" -gt "$ALERT_THRESHOLD_CPU" ]; then
log_message "warning" "High CPU usage for $process_name: ${cpu_usage}%"
fi
if [ "$mem_usage" -gt "$ALERT_THRESHOLD_MEM" ]; then
log_message "warning" "High memory usage for $process_name: ${mem_usage}%"
fi
if [ "$runtime_seconds" -gt "$ALERT_THRESHOLD_TIME" ]; then
log_message "warning" "Process $process_name has been running for ${runtime_seconds} seconds"
fi
}
```

Creating Self-Healing Systems

Self-healing automation systems can automatically detect, diagnose, and resolve common issues without human intervention. These systems implement intelligent response mechanisms that can restart failed services, clear resource bottlenecks, update configurations, and even modify scheduling parameters based on observed conditions. The goal is creating resilient automation that maintains security coverage even when individual components experience problems.

Implementing self-healing capabilities requires careful balance between automated recovery and human oversight. While automation can handle routine failures and well-understood issues, more complex problems might require human analysis to prevent automated responses from causing additional issues. Effective self-healing systems include safeguards that prevent infinite recovery loops and escalation procedures that engage human administrators when automated recovery attempts fail.

Health Check Integration and Reporting

Comprehensive health check systems provide regular assessment of automation framework components, dependencies, and overall system status. These health checks should evaluate not only the technical functionality of automated systems but also their security effectiveness, compliance with policies, and alignment with current threat landscapes. Regular health reporting enables proactive maintenance and continuous improvement of security automation capabilities.

Health check integration involves connecting monitoring data from various sources including system metrics, application logs, security event data, and external service status. This integrated approach provides holistic visibility into automation health and enables correlation analysis that might reveal issues not apparent when examining individual components in isolation. Automated health reporting should provide both real-time status information and trend analysis that supports long-term planning and optimization efforts.

Advanced Cron Techniques for Security Automation

Advanced cron techniques enable sophisticated security automation scenarios that go beyond basic scheduling. These techniques include dynamic scheduling based on threat levels, conditional execution based on system state, distributed scheduling across multiple systems, and integration with external event sources. Mastering these advanced techniques allows security professionals to create adaptive automation frameworks that respond intelligently to changing security conditions.

Dynamic scheduling involves modifying cron schedules based on current threat levels, system load, or other relevant conditions. This approach enables more frequent security scans during high-threat periods while reducing automation overhead during normal operations. Implementing dynamic scheduling requires careful integration between threat detection systems and cron management, ensuring that schedule modifications don't create gaps in security coverage.

Conditional Execution and Smart Scheduling

Smart scheduling techniques enable cron jobs to make intelligent decisions about whether and how to execute based on current system conditions. Rather than blindly following predetermined schedules, smart automation can assess system load, network conditions, security alerts, and other factors before deciding whether to proceed with scheduled tasks. This intelligence prevents automation from interfering with critical operations while maintaining security coverage.

Implementing conditional execution requires building intelligence into scripts that can assess relevant conditions and make appropriate decisions. This might involve checking system load averages, verifying network connectivity, consulting threat intelligence feeds, or coordinating with other automation systems. The key is creating decision logic that maintains security effectiveness while adapting to dynamic operational conditions.

Distributed Coordination and Load Balancing

Large-scale security automation often requires coordination across multiple systems to distribute workload and ensure comprehensive coverage. This distributed approach might involve coordinating vulnerability scans across different network segments, distributing log analysis tasks among multiple servers, or implementing failover mechanisms that ensure critical security functions continue even when individual systems experience problems.

Implementing distributed coordination requires developing communication mechanisms between automation systems, creating shared state management, and establishing conflict resolution procedures. Technologies like distributed locking, message queuing, and centralized configuration management enable robust distributed automation that can scale with organizational needs while maintaining consistency and reliability.

Troubleshooting and Optimization

Effective troubleshooting of cron-based security automation requires systematic approaches to identifying, diagnosing, and resolving issues that can affect automated security processes. Common problems include environment differences between interactive and cron execution contexts, resource conflicts between competing processes, timing issues that cause script failures, and integration problems with external services. Developing robust troubleshooting methodologies ensures that automation issues can be resolved quickly before they impact security coverage.

Performance optimization of security automation involves analyzing execution patterns, identifying bottlenecks, and implementing improvements that enhance both speed and reliability. This optimization process should consider not only individual script performance but also the overall impact of automation on system resources and the effectiveness of security coverage. Regular performance analysis enables continuous improvement of automation frameworks.

Common Cron Issues and Solutions

Environmental differences between interactive shells and cron execution contexts cause many automation failures. Interactive shells inherit complex environments with custom PATH settings, aliases, functions, and environment variables that cron jobs don't automatically receive. Solving these issues requires either explicitly setting required environment variables within scripts or using absolute paths for all external commands.

Timing-related issues represent another common category of cron problems. Scripts that depend on specific system states, network services, or external resources might fail if those dependencies aren't available at execution time. Implementing retry logic, dependency checking, and graceful degradation helps create more resilient automation that can handle temporary resource unavailability.

Performance Monitoring and Optimization

Continuous performance monitoring of security automation provides insights into resource utilization patterns, execution trends, and optimization opportunities. This monitoring should track metrics such as execution time, resource consumption, success rates, and error patterns across all automated security tasks. Analyzing these metrics over time reveals trends that can guide optimization efforts and capacity planning.

Optimization strategies for security automation include parallelization of independent tasks, caching of frequently accessed data, optimization of script logic and external command usage, and intelligent scheduling that minimizes resource conflicts. The goal is maximizing security coverage while minimizing impact on system performance and user productivity.

Conclusion

The integration of cron scheduling with Bash scripting creates powerful automation capabilities that form the backbone of modern cybersecurity operations. Through systematic application of time-based scheduling, comprehensive logging and monitoring, and intelligent design of security automation scripts, organizations can maintain consistent security postures that operate effectively around the clock. The techniques and strategies covered in this chapter provide the foundation for building robust, scalable security automation frameworks that adapt to evolving threats while maintaining operational efficiency.

Successful implementation of cron-based security automation requires careful attention to security considerations, comprehensive monitoring and logging, and continuous optimization based on operational experience. The watchdog systems and health checks discussed in this chapter ensure that automation remains reliable and effective, while advanced techniques enable sophisticated scenarios that can adapt to changing security conditions. As cybersecurity threats continue to evolve in complexity and frequency, the ability to implement effective automated responses becomes increasingly critical for maintaining strong security postures.

The journey from basic cron scheduling to sophisticated security automation frameworks represents a significant capability enhancement for any cybersecurity professional. By mastering these techniques and continuously refining automation strategies based on operational feedback, security teams can achieve levels of coverage and responsiveness that would be impossible through manual processes alone. The investment in building robust automation capabilities pays dividends in improved security effectiveness, reduced operational overhead, and enhanced ability to respond to emerging threats in today's dynamic cybersecurity landscape.

Chapter 8: Building Your Own Bash Security Toolkit

The culmination of mastering Bash for cybersecurity lies in creating your own comprehensive security toolkit that combines all the techniques, methodologies, and best practices learned throughout this journey. Building a modular, extensible security toolkit represents more than just assembling individual scripts; it involves architecting a cohesive framework that can grow and adapt to meet evolving security challenges. This chapter guides you through the process of designing, implementing, and deploying a professional-grade Bash-based security toolkit that rivals commercial solutions while maintaining the flexibility and transparency that open-source tools provide.

Creating your own security toolkit offers numerous advantages over relying solely on existing tools. Custom toolkits can be tailored to your specific environment, organizational needs, and security requirements. They provide complete visibility into functionality, enabling security professionals to understand exactly what each component does and how it operates. Additionally, building your own toolkit develops deep technical expertise that enhances your ability to adapt and extend security capabilities as new threats and technologies emerge.

The process of building a comprehensive security toolkit requires careful planning, modular design principles, and attention to user experience. The toolkit must be robust enough for production use while remaining maintainable and extensible. This chapter demonstrates how to create a pentesting suite that serves as both a practical tool and a learning platform, incorporating industry best practices for security tool development and deployment.

Project: Build a Modular Bash-Based Pentesting Suite

Developing a modular pentesting suite requires architectural decisions that will influence the toolkit's scalability, maintainability, and usability for years to come. The foundation of any successful security toolkit lies in its modular design, which enables individual components to be developed, tested, and maintained independently while working together seamlessly. This modular approach facilitates collaborative development, simplifies troubleshooting, and allows for incremental improvements without disrupting the entire framework.

The pentesting suite should encompass core security testing capabilities including reconnaissance, vulnerability scanning, exploitation assistance, and post-exploitation tasks. Each module within the suite should follow consistent interfaces and conventions while maintaining the flexibility to implement specialized functionality. The architecture must balance ease of use for beginners with the power and flexibility that experienced penetration testers require for complex engagements.

Designing the Toolkit Architecture

The architectural foundation of your pentesting suite determines its long-term viability and extensibility. A well-designed architecture separates concerns appropriately, providing clear interfaces between components while maintaining loose coupling that allows individual modules to evolve independently. The core architecture should include a central framework that manages module loading, configuration, logging, and inter-module communication, surrounded by specialized modules that implement specific security testing capabilities.

Implementing a plugin-based architecture enables the toolkit to grow organically as new security testing needs arise. This architecture should define standard interfaces for modules, including initialization procedures, configuration management, execution contexts, and result reporting. The framework should handle common tasks such as target validation, credential management, output formatting, and error handling, allowing individual modules to focus on their specific security testing functionality.

The directory structure of your toolkit should reflect its modular architecture, with clear separation between core framework components, individual modules, configuration files, documentation, and supporting resources. A typical structure might include directories for core libraries, individual security modules, configuration templates, output formatting components, documentation, and example usage scenarios. This organization facilitates both development and deployment while making the toolkit accessible to users with varying levels of Bash expertise.

```
pentesting-suite/
├── core/
│   ├── framework.sh # Core framework functions
│   ├── config.sh # Configuration management
│   ├── logger.sh # Logging infrastructure
│   └── utils.sh # Common utilities
├── modules/
│   ├── reconnaissance/
│   │   ├── nmap_scanner.sh
│   │   ├── dns_enum.sh
│   │   └── web_discovery.sh
│   ├── vulnerability/
│   │   ├── web_vulns.sh
│   │   ├── network_vulns.sh
│   │   └── service_vulns.sh
│   └── exploitation/
│   ├── web_exploits.sh
│   └── network_exploits.sh
├── config/
│   ├── default.conf
│   └── templates/
├── output/
│   ├── formatters/
│   └── reports/
│
```

```
├── docs/
└── examples/
```

Implementing Core Framework Components

The core framework serves as the backbone of your pentesting suite, providing essential services that all modules can leverage. This framework should implement common functionality such as configuration management, logging, error handling, progress reporting, and module lifecycle management. By centralizing these capabilities, individual modules can focus on their specific security testing logic while maintaining consistency across the entire toolkit.

Configuration management within the framework should support multiple configuration sources including command-line arguments, configuration files, environment variables, and interactive prompts. The system should implement a hierarchical configuration approach where command-line arguments override configuration file settings, which in turn override default values. This flexibility enables the toolkit to adapt to different usage scenarios while maintaining sensible defaults for common operations.

The logging infrastructure should provide multiple output levels and destinations, enabling detailed debugging information during development while providing clean, professional output for production use. The logging system should support structured logging formats that facilitate automated analysis while remaining human-readable for manual review. Additionally, the framework should implement progress reporting capabilities that keep users informed during long-running operations without overwhelming them with unnecessary detail.

```
#!/bin/bash
# Core framework initialization and module management
TOOLKIT_ROOT="$(cd "$(dirname "${BASH_SOURCE[0]}")" && pwd)"
MODULES_DIR="$TOOLKIT_ROOT/modules"
CONFIG_DIR="$TOOLKIT_ROOT/config"
```

```
OUTPUT_DIR="$TOOLKIT_ROOT/output"
# Source core components
source "$TOOLKIT_ROOT/core/config.sh"
source "$TOOLKIT_ROOT/core/logger.sh"
source "$TOOLKIT_ROOT/core/utils.sh"
# Initialize framework
initialize_framework() {
log_info "Initializing pentesting suite framework"
# Load configuration
load_configuration "$CONFIG_DIR/default.conf"
# Validate environment
validate_environment
# Initialize output directories
prepare_output_directories
log_info "Framework initialization complete"
}
# Module management functions
load_module() {
local module_name="$1"
local module_path="$MODULES_DIR/$module_name"
if [ ! -f "$module_path" ]; then
log_error "Module not found: $module_name"
return 1
fi
log_debug "Loading module: $module_name"
source "$module_path"
# Verify module implements required functions
if ! declare -f "${module_name}_init" >/dev/null; then
log_error "Module $module_name missing required init function"
return 1
fi
# Initialize module
"${module_name}_init"
log_info "Module loaded successfully: $module_name"
}
```

Creating Specialized Security Modules

Individual security modules implement specific testing capabilities while adhering to the framework's interface specifications. Each module should be self-contained, implementing its own initialization, execution, and cleanup procedures while leveraging the core framework for common services. Modules should be designed with reusability in mind, accepting standardized input formats and producing consistent output that can be consumed by other modules or external tools.

Reconnaissance modules form the foundation of most penetration testing engagements, gathering information about target systems, networks, and applications. These modules should implement various discovery techniques including network scanning, service enumeration, web application discovery, and information gathering from public sources. The modules should be capable of operating in both active and passive modes, allowing penetration testers to choose appropriate levels of detectability based on engagement requirements.

Vulnerability assessment modules build upon reconnaissance results to identify potential security weaknesses in discovered systems and services. These modules should implement both automated scanning capabilities and manual testing procedures, providing comprehensive coverage of common vulnerability categories. The modules should integrate with vulnerability databases and provide detailed information about identified issues, including severity ratings, exploitation guidance, and remediation recommendations.

```
#!/bin/bash
# Example reconnaissance module implementation
nmap_scanner_init() {
log_debug "Initializing nmap scanner module"
# Verify nmap availability
if ! command -v nmap >/dev/null 2>&1; then
log_error "nmap not found in PATH"
return 1
```

```
fi
# Set module defaults
NMAP_SCAN_TYPE="${NMAP_SCAN_TYPE:-SYN}"
NMAP_TIMING="${NMAP_TIMING:-T4}"
NMAP_OUTPUT_FORMAT="${NMAP_OUTPUT_FORMAT:-xml}"
log_info "Nmap scanner module initialized"
}
nmap_scanner_execute() {
local target="$1"
local scan_type="$2"
local output_file="$3"
log_info "Starting nmap scan of target: $target"
# Build nmap command based on scan type
local nmap_cmd="nmap"
case "$scan_type" in
"quick")
nmap_cmd="$nmap_cmd -sS -T4—top-ports 1000"
;;
"full")
nmap_cmd="$nmap_cmd -sS -T4 -p-"
;;
"stealth")
nmap_cmd="$nmap_cmd -sS -T2 -f"
;;
*)
log_error "Unknown scan type: $scan_type"
return 1
;;
esac
# Add output formatting
nmap_cmd="$nmap_cmd -oX $output_file"
# Execute scan
log_debug "Executing: $nmap_cmd $target"
eval "$nmap_cmd $target"
if [ $? -eq 0 ]; then
log_info "Nmap scan completed successfully"
parse_nmap_results "$output_file"
else
log_error "Nmap scan failed"
```

```
return 1
fi
}
```

Implementing Inter-Module Communication

Effective inter-module communication enables complex testing workflows that combine multiple security testing techniques. The framework should provide standardized mechanisms for modules to share data, coordinate activities, and build upon each other's results. This communication infrastructure should support both synchronous and asynchronous interactions while maintaining clear separation between module implementations.

Data sharing between modules should use standardized formats that enable seamless information flow throughout the testing process. Common data structures might include target lists, discovered services, identified vulnerabilities, and exploitation results. The framework should provide utilities for converting between different data formats and validating data integrity as information flows between modules.

Workflow coordination becomes particularly important when implementing complex testing scenarios that require specific sequencing of security testing activities. The framework should support dependency management that ensures prerequisite modules complete successfully before dependent modules execute. Additionally, the system should provide mechanisms for conditional execution based on previous module results and dynamic workflow modification based on discovered information.

Adding User Options, Menus, and Output Formatting

Creating an intuitive user interface significantly impacts the usability and adoption of your security toolkit. While command-line tools typically rely on arguments and flags for configuration, adding interactive menus and guided workflows makes the toolkit accessible to users with varying levels of experience. The user interface should accommodate both interactive usage and automated execution, providing flexibility for different operational scenarios.

Effective user interface design for security tools balances ease of use with the precision and control that security professionals require. Interactive menus should guide users through complex configuration options while providing shortcuts for experienced users who prefer direct command-line access. The interface should provide clear feedback about ongoing operations, estimated completion times, and any issues that require user attention.

Designing Interactive Menus and Workflows

Interactive menu systems provide guided access to toolkit functionality while reducing the complexity of remembering specific command-line arguments and options. Well-designed menus organize functionality logically, provide clear descriptions of available options, and guide users through complex configuration processes. The menu system should support both novice users who need guidance and experienced users who want quick access to specific functionality.

Menu design should follow consistent patterns that users can learn and apply across different sections of the toolkit. Common patterns include hierarchical menus for organizing related functionality, input validation that prevents invalid configurations, and confirmation prompts for potentially destructive operations. The menu system should maintain state appropriately, allowing users to build complex configurations incrementally without losing previous selections.

Dynamic menu generation enables the toolkit to adapt its interface based on available modules, current configuration, and discovered target information. This adaptability ensures that users only see relevant options while maintaining a clean, uncluttered interface. The menu system should also support batch operations that allow users to configure multiple targets or testing scenarios efficiently.

```
#!/bin/bash
# Interactive menu system implementation
show_main_menu() {
clear
echo
"╔══════════════════════════════════════════════════════════════════════════════════╗"
echo "║ Bash Security Toolkit ║"
echo "║ Main Menu ║"
echo
"╚══════════════════════════════════════════════════════════════════════════════════╝"
echo
echo "1) Reconnaissance"
echo "2) Vulnerability Assessment"
echo "3) Exploitation"
echo "4) Post-Exploitation"
echo "5) Reporting"
echo "6) Configuration"
echo "7) Help"
echo "0) Exit"
echo
read -p "Please select an option [0-7]: " choice
case $choice in
1) show_reconnaissance_menu ;;
2) show_vulnerability_menu ;;
3) show_exploitation_menu ;;
4) show_post_exploitation_menu ;;
5) show_reporting_menu ;;
6) show_configuration_menu ;;
7) show_help ;;
0) exit 0 ;;
*)
echo "Invalid option. Please try again."
sleep 2
show_main_menu
;;
esac
}
```

```
show_reconnaissance_menu() {
clear
echo
"╔══════════════════════════════════════════════════════════════════════════
══════════════════════════════════════════════╗"
echo "║ Reconnaissance Menu ║"
echo
"╚══════════════════════════════════════════════════════════════════════════
══════════════════════════════════════════════╝"
echo
echo "1) Network Discovery"
echo "2) Port Scanning"
echo "3) Service Enumeration"
echo "4) Web Application Discovery"
echo "5) DNS Enumeration"
echo "6) OSINT Gathering"
echo "7) Full Reconnaissance Suite"
echo "0) Back to Main Menu"
echo
read -p "Please select an option [0-7]: " choice
case $choice in
1) run_network_discovery ;;
2) run_port_scanning ;;
3) run_service_enumeration ;;
4) run_web_discovery ;;
5) run_dns_enumeration ;;
6) run_osint_gathering ;;
7) run_full_reconnaissance ;;
0) show_main_menu ;;
*)
echo "Invalid option. Please try again."
sleep 2
show_reconnaissance_menu
;;
esac
}
```

Implementing Command-Line Argument Processing

Robust command-line argument processing enables power users to access toolkit functionality directly while maintaining compatibility with automated scripts and workflows. The argument processing system should support both short and long option formats, provide comprehensive help information, and implement intelligent defaults that minimize required configuration. Advanced argument processing should support configuration files, environment variable integration, and complex parameter validation.

Argument parsing should handle complex scenarios including conflicting options, dependent parameters, and conditional requirements. The system should provide clear error messages when invalid combinations are specified and suggest correct usage patterns. Additionally, the argument processor should support batch operations, configuration templating, and integration with external configuration management systems.

The command-line interface should support common Unix conventions including support for standard input and output redirection, pipeline compatibility, and appropriate exit codes. This compatibility ensures that the toolkit integrates seamlessly with existing security workflows and automation frameworks. The interface should also support verbose and quiet modes that adjust output detail based on user preferences and operational requirements.

```
#!/bin/bash
# Advanced command-line argument processing
process_arguments() {
local OPTS=$(getopt -o ht:m:v:q—long help,target:,module:,verbose:,quiet,config: -n 'security-toolkit'—"$@")
if [ $? != 0 ]; then
echo "Failed parsing options." >&2
exit 1
fi
eval set—"$OPTS"
while true; do
```

```
case "$1" in
-h |—help)
show_usage
exit 0
;;
-t |—target)
TARGET="$2"
shift 2
;;
-m |—module)
MODULE="$2"
validate_module "$MODULE"
shift 2
;;
-v |—verbose)
VERBOSE_LEVEL="$2"
shift 2
;;
-q |—quiet)
QUIET_MODE=true
shift
;;
—config)
CONFIG_FILE="$2"
load_configuration "$CONFIG_FILE"
shift 2
;;
—)
shift
break
;;
*)
echo "Internal error!"
exit 1
;;
esac
done
# Validate required arguments
if [ -z "$TARGET" ] && [ "$MODULE" != "help" ]; then
```

```
echo "Error: Target is required"
show_usage
exit 1
fi
}
```

Creating Professional Output Formatting

Professional output formatting enhances the usability and credibility of your security toolkit while ensuring that results can be easily interpreted by both human analysts and automated systems. The formatting system should support multiple output formats including console display, structured data formats, and professional reports. Each format should be optimized for its intended audience and use case while maintaining consistency in information presentation.

Console output formatting should use appropriate colors, indentation, and visual elements to highlight important information and create clear information hierarchy. The formatting should be configurable to accommodate different terminal capabilities and user preferences. Progress indicators, status messages, and result summaries should provide clear feedback about toolkit operations without overwhelming users with excessive detail.

Structured output formats such as JSON, XML, and CSV enable integration with external analysis tools and automated workflows. These formats should include comprehensive metadata about the testing process, including timestamps, tool versions, configuration parameters, and data quality indicators. The structured output should be schema-compliant where applicable and include appropriate validation to ensure data integrity.

```
#!/bin/bash
# Output formatting system
# Color definitions for console output
RED='\033[0;31m'
GREEN='\033[0;32m'
YELLOW='\033[1;33m'
```

```
BLUE='\033[0;34m'
PURPLE='\033[0;35m'
CYAN='\033[0;36m'
WHITE='\033[1;37m'
NC='\033[0m' # No Color
# Formatting functions
print_header() {
local title="$1"
local width=${2:-60}
echo -e "${BLUE}$(printf '═%.0s' $(seq 1 $width))${NC}"
printf "${BLUE}║${WHITE}%*s${BLUE}║${NC}\n"
$(((${#title}+$width-2)/2)) "$title"
echo -e "${BLUE}$(printf '═%.0s' $(seq 1 $width))${NC}"
}
print_section() {
local title="$1"
echo -e "\n${CYAN}▸ $title${NC}"
echo -e "${CYAN}$(printf '─%.0s' $(seq 1 ${#title}))${NC}"
}
print_result() {
local status="$1"
local message="$2"
case "$status" in
"success")
echo -e " ${GREEN}✓${NC} $message"
;;
"warning")
echo -e " ${YELLOW}⚠${NC} $message"
;;
"error")
echo -e " ${RED}✗${NC} $message"
;;
"info")
echo -e " ${BLUE}ℹ${NC} $message"
;;
esac
}
# JSON output formatting
format_json_output() {
```

```
local data="$1"
local output_file="$2"
cat > "$output_file" << EOF
{
"toolkit_version": "$TOOLKIT_VERSION",
"scan_timestamp": "$(date -u +%Y-%m-%dT%H:%M:%SZ)",
"target": "$TARGET",
"results": $data
}
EOF
}
```

Progress Tracking and Status Updates

Implementing comprehensive progress tracking keeps users informed during long-running security operations while providing valuable diagnostic information when issues occur. The progress tracking system should provide estimated completion times, current operation status, and performance metrics that help users understand toolkit behavior. Advanced progress tracking should support parallel operations and provide aggregate status across multiple concurrent activities.

Real-time status updates should balance informativeness with performance, providing meaningful feedback without significantly impacting operation speed. The status system should support different verbosity levels, allowing users to choose between minimal progress indicators and detailed operational logging. Additionally, the system should provide mechanisms for pausing, resuming, and canceling long-running operations gracefully.

Performance metrics collection during toolkit execution provides valuable information for optimization and troubleshooting. Metrics should include operation timing, resource utilization, success rates, and error frequencies. This information enables continuous improvement of toolkit performance and helps identify potential issues before they impact security testing effectiveness.

Packaging and Sharing Your Toolkit

Professional packaging and distribution of your security toolkit ensures that it can be easily deployed, maintained, and shared across different environments and user communities. Effective packaging addresses dependency management, installation procedures, configuration management, and update mechanisms. The packaging approach should accommodate different deployment scenarios including standalone installations, containerized deployments, and integration with existing security frameworks.

Creating a distributable toolkit involves more than simply archiving script files. Professional packaging includes comprehensive documentation, installation scripts, dependency management, configuration templates, and automated testing procedures. The package should include version information, licensing details, and support information that enables users to deploy and maintain the toolkit effectively.

Creating Installation and Setup Scripts

Automated installation scripts simplify toolkit deployment while ensuring consistent configuration across different environments. Installation scripts should handle dependency verification, directory structure creation, permission configuration, and initial setup procedures. The scripts should be robust enough to handle various operating system configurations while providing clear feedback about installation progress and any issues that require attention.

Dependency management represents a critical aspect of toolkit installation, as security tools often rely on numerous external utilities and libraries. The installation script should verify the availability of required dependencies, provide installation guidance for missing components, and offer alternative configurations when specific tools are unavailable. The system should support both automatic dependency installation where possible and manual installation guidance for more complex requirements.

Configuration management during installation should establish sensible defaults while providing mechanisms for customization based on specific environment requirements. The installation process should create necessary configuration files, establish appropriate file permissions, and initialize logging and output directories. Additionally, the installer should provide options for different installation types including development installations with full debugging capabilities and production installations optimized for performance.

```
#!/bin/bash
# Toolkit installation script
TOOLKIT_NAME="Bash Security Toolkit"
TOOLKIT_VERSION="1.0.0"
INSTALL_DIR="/opt/bash-security-toolkit"
CONFIG_DIR="/etc/bash-security-toolkit"
LOG_DIR="/var/log/bash-security-toolkit"
install_toolkit() {
echo "Installing $TOOLKIT_NAME v$TOOLKIT_VERSION"
echo "========================================"
# Check for root privileges
if [ "$EUID" -ne 0 ]; then
echo "Error: Installation requires root privileges"
exit 1
fi
# Verify system requirements
verify_system_requirements
# Check dependencies
check_dependencies
# Create directories
create_directories
# Copy files
install_files
# Set permissions
configure_permissions
# Create configuration
```

```
setup_configuration
# Register with system
register_toolkit
echo "Installation completed successfully!"
echo "Run 'bash-security-toolkit—help' to get started"
}
verify_system_requirements() {
echo "Verifying system requirements..."
# Check operating system
if ! [[ "$OSTYPE" == "linux-gnu"* ]]; then
echo "Warning: This toolkit is optimized for Linux systems"
fi
# Check Bash version
if [ "${BASH_VERSION%%.*}" -lt 4 ]; then
echo "Error: Bash 4.0 or higher is required"
exit 1
fi
# Check available disk space
local available_space=$(df /opt | awk 'NR==2 {print $4}')
if [ "$available_space" -lt 100000 ]; then
echo "Warning: Low disk space available"
fi
echo "System requirements verified"
}
check_dependencies() {
echo "Checking dependencies..."
local required_tools=("nmap" "curl" "jq" "xmllint" "openssl")
local missing_tools=()
for tool in "${required_tools[@]}"; do
if ! command -v "$tool" >/dev/null 2>&1; then
missing_tools+=("$tool")
fi
done
if [ ${#missing_tools[@]} -gt 0 ]; then
echo "Missing required tools: ${missing_tools[*]}"
echo "Please install these tools before continuing"
exit 1
fi
echo "All dependencies satisfied"
```

```
}
```

Documentation and User Guides

Comprehensive documentation ensures that users can effectively deploy, configure, and operate your security toolkit. Documentation should include installation guides, configuration references, usage examples, troubleshooting information, and development guidance for extending toolkit functionality. Well-structured documentation reduces support burden while enabling users to maximize the toolkit's capabilities.

User guides should be organized by skill level and use case, providing quick-start guides for beginners alongside comprehensive reference materials for advanced users. The documentation should include practical examples that demonstrate common security testing scenarios while explaining the underlying concepts and methodologies. Interactive tutorials and guided exercises help users develop proficiency with toolkit features and security testing techniques.

Technical documentation should cover toolkit architecture, module development guidelines, API references, and extension mechanisms. This documentation enables other developers to contribute to toolkit development and create custom modules that integrate seamlessly with the existing framework. Code documentation should follow established standards and include examples that illustrate proper usage patterns and best practices.

Version Control and Release Management

Professional version control and release management practices ensure that toolkit development can scale effectively while maintaining quality and stability. Version control should track not only code changes but also configuration updates, documentation revisions, and test results. The version control strategy should support collaborative development while maintaining clear audit trails for all changes.

Release management involves coordinating code changes, testing procedures, documentation updates, and distribution processes. Each release should undergo comprehensive testing that verifies functionality across different operating systems and configurations. The release process should include automated testing, security scanning, and validation procedures that ensure release quality and reliability.

Branching strategies should support both stable releases and ongoing development activities. The strategy should enable hotfix releases for critical security issues while maintaining long-term development branches for major feature additions. Additionally, the version control system should support tagged releases that enable users to deploy specific toolkit versions consistently across different environments.

Community Building and Contribution Guidelines

Building a user and developer community around your toolkit accelerates development while improving tool quality through diverse testing and feedback. Community building involves creating communication channels, establishing contribution guidelines, and recognizing valuable contributions from community members. Effective community management balances openness with quality control, ensuring that contributions enhance rather than compromise toolkit capabilities.

Contribution guidelines should clearly define processes for reporting issues, suggesting enhancements, and submitting code changes. The guidelines should include coding standards, testing requirements, and documentation expectations that maintain consistency across contributions. Additionally, the guidelines should address security considerations for contributed code, including review procedures and approval processes for security-sensitive changes.

Recognition and acknowledgment of community contributions encourage ongoing participation while building reputation for both individual contributors and the toolkit project. This recognition might include contributor lists, achievement systems, and opportunities for community members to take leadership roles in specific areas of toolkit development.

Integrating with Python and Other Tools

Modern security toolkits increasingly rely on integration with multiple programming languages and external tools to provide comprehensive capabilities that would be difficult to implement in any single language. Python integration offers value for security toolkits due to Python's extensive library ecosystem, strong community support, and excellent capabilities for data analysis and visualization. Effective integration maintains the performance and simplicity advantages of Bash while leveraging specialized capabilities from other tools.

Integration strategies should preserve the modularity and independence of individual components while enabling seamless data flow and coordination between different tools and languages. The integration framework should handle data format conversions, error propagation, and performance optimization across language boundaries. Additionally, the integration should support both synchronous and asynchronous execution patterns based on operational requirements.

Designing Multi-Language Architectures

Multi-language architectures enable security toolkits to leverage the strengths of different programming languages while maintaining cohesive user experiences and consistent data handling. The architecture should define clear interfaces and communication protocols that enable components written in different languages to work together effectively. These interfaces should be language-agnostic, using standard data formats and communication mechanisms that can be implemented across different technology stacks.

Data serialization and communication protocols form the backbone of multi-language integration. Common approaches include JSON for structured data exchange, REST APIs for service communication, and message queues for asynchronous coordination. The chosen protocols should balance performance with simplicity, ensuring that integration overhead doesn't significantly impact toolkit operation speed while maintaining reliability and error handling capabilities.

Process management becomes more complex in multi-language environments, requiring coordination of different runtime environments, dependency management systems, and execution contexts. The toolkit should provide utilities for managing Python virtual environments, handling Node.js dependencies, and coordinating with system-level tools. This management should be transparent to users while providing developers with the flexibility to leverage appropriate tools for specific tasks.

```
#!/bin/bash
# Multi-language integration framework
# Python integration functions
execute_python_module() {
local module_name="$1"
local input_data="$2"
local output_file="$3"
# Verify Python environment
if ! verify_python_environment; then
log_error "Python environment not properly configured"
return 1
fi
# Prepare input data
local temp_input=$(mktemp)
echo "$input_data" > "$temp_input"
# Execute Python module
python3 "$TOOLKIT_ROOT/python_modules/$module_name.py" \
```

```
—input "$temp_input" \
—output "$output_file" \
—config "$CONFIG_FILE"
local exit_code=$?
rm -f "$temp_input"
if [ $exit_code -eq 0 ]; then
log_info "Python module $module_name executed successfully"
else
log_error "Python module $module_name failed with exit code $exit_code"
fi
return $exit_code
}
verify_python_environment() {
# Check Python availability
if ! command -v python3 >/dev/null 2>&1; then
log_error "Python 3 not found"
return 1
fi
# Verify virtual environment if configured
if [ -n "$PYTHON_VENV" ]; then
if [ ! -f "$PYTHON_VENV/bin/activate" ]; then
log_error "Python virtual environment not found: $PYTHON_VENV"
return 1
fi
source "$PYTHON_VENV/bin/activate"
fi
# Check required Python packages
local required_packages=("requests" "beautifulsoup4" "cryptography")
for package in "${required_packages[@]}"; do
if ! python3 -c "import $package" 2>/dev/null; then
log_error "Required Python package not found: $package"
return 1
fi
done
return 0
}
```

Python Integration for Advanced Analytics

Python's extensive ecosystem of data analysis and machine learning libraries provides powerful capabilities that complement Bash's system-level strengths. Integration with Python enables advanced analytics including pattern recognition in security logs, behavioral analysis of network traffic, and automated threat intelligence correlation. These capabilities significantly enhance the analytical power of your security toolkit while maintaining the simplicity and performance of Bash for core operations.

Data pipeline integration between Bash and Python should support streaming data processing for real-time analysis alongside batch processing for comprehensive historical analysis. The integration should handle large datasets efficiently, implementing appropriate chunking, caching, and memory management strategies. Additionally, the pipeline should support incremental processing that can resume from interruption points and handle partial data updates effectively.

Visualization capabilities through Python libraries like matplotlib, plotly, and seaborn enable the creation of professional security reports with charts, graphs, and interactive visualizations. The integration should support both automated report generation and interactive exploration of security data. These visualization capabilities transform raw security data into actionable intelligence that can be easily understood by stakeholders at different technical levels.

Machine learning integration through Python enables predictive security analytics that can identify emerging threats and anomalous behaviors before they cause significant damage. These capabilities include anomaly detection in network traffic, predictive modeling for vulnerability assessment, and automated classification of security events. The machine learning components should be designed to operate with minimal manual tuning while providing transparency into their decision-making processes.

```
#!/usr/bin/env python3
```

```
# Example Python module for log analysis
import json
import sys
import argparse
import pandas as pd
import matplotlib.pyplot as plt
from collections import Counter
from datetime import datetime, timedelta
class SecurityLogAnalyzer:
def __init__(self, config_file=None):
self.config = self.load_config(config_file) if config_file else {}
self.analysis_results = {}
def load_config(self, config_file):
"""Load configuration from file"""
try:
with open(config_file, 'r') as f:
return json.load(f)
except Exception as e:
print(f"Warning: Could not load config file: {e}")
return {}
def analyze_failed_logins(self, log_data):
"""Analyze failed login patterns"""
failed_logins = []
for entry in log_data:
if 'failed' in entry.get('message', '').lower():
failed_logins.append({
'timestamp': entry.get('timestamp'),
'ip': entry.get('source_ip'),
'user': entry.get('username')
})
# Identify brute force attempts
ip_counts = Counter([login['ip'] for login in failed_logins])
brute_force_ips = {ip: count for ip, count in ip_counts.items()
if count > self.config.get('brute_force_threshold', 10)}
self.analysis_results['failed_logins'] = {
'total_attempts': len(failed_logins),
'unique_ips': len(ip_counts),
'brute_force_ips': brute_force_ips
}
```

```
return self.analysis_results['failed_logins']
def generate_report(self, output_file):
"""Generate comprehensive security report"""
report = {
'analysis_timestamp': datetime.now().isoformat(),
'results': self.analysis_results
}
with open(output_file, 'w') as f:
json.dump(report, f, indent=2)
print(f"Analysis report generated: {output_file}")
if __name__ == "__main__":
parser = argparse.ArgumentParser(description='Security Log Analyzer')
parser.add_argument('—input', required=True, help='Input log file')
parser.add_argument('—output', required=True, help='Output report file')
parser.add_argument('—config', help='Configuration file')
args = parser.parse_args()
# Initialize analyzer
analyzer = SecurityLogAnalyzer(args.config)
# Load and analyze log data
with open(args.input, 'r') as f:
log_data = json.load(f)
analyzer.analyze_failed_logins(log_data)
analyzer.generate_report(args.output)
```

Chapter 9: Real-World Case Studies and Use Cases

The theoretical knowledge and practical skills developed throughout this book find their true validation in real-world cybersecurity environments where security professionals rely on Bash scripting to solve complex challenges, automate critical processes, and respond to evolving threats. This chapter examines how security teams across different organizational contexts leverage Bash scripting to enhance their operational effectiveness, drawing from actual case studies and proven methodologies that demonstrate the practical value of shell scripting expertise in modern cybersecurity operations.

Understanding how Bash scripting integrates into real-world security workflows provides essential context for applying the techniques learned in previous chapters. Security professionals operate in diverse environments with varying constraints, requirements, and threat landscapes, yet common patterns emerge in how successful teams utilize scripting to overcome operational challenges. These patterns reveal not only the technical applications of Bash scripting but also the strategic thinking and problem-solving approaches that distinguish effective security practitioners.

The evolution of cybersecurity operations has increasingly emphasized automation, scalability, and rapid response capabilities that align perfectly with Bash scripting strengths. As organizations face growing volumes of security data, expanding attack surfaces, and sophisticated threat actors, the ability to quickly develop and deploy custom automation solutions becomes a critical competitive advantage. This chapter explores how security teams translate business requirements into effective scripting solutions while maintaining the agility needed to adapt to changing threat landscapes.

How Security Teams Use Bash in Practice

Modern security operations centers represent complex ecosystems where multiple tools, technologies, and processes must work together seamlessly to provide comprehensive security coverage. Bash scripting serves as the connective tissue that binds these disparate elements into cohesive workflows, enabling security teams to automate routine tasks, orchestrate complex procedures, and respond rapidly to emerging threats. The practical application of Bash in these environments demonstrates both the versatility of shell scripting and the creative problem-solving capabilities of security professionals.

Security teams typically employ Bash scripting across three primary domains: operational automation that handles routine security tasks, incident response automation that accelerates threat mitigation, and analytical automation that processes large volumes of security data to extract actionable intelligence. Each domain presents unique challenges and requirements that influence scripting approaches, design decisions, and implementation strategies. Understanding these domains provides essential context for developing effective security automation solutions.

Enterprise SOC Operations and Workflow Integration

Enterprise Security Operations Centers represent some of the most demanding environments for Bash scripting applications, where scripts must operate reliably at scale while integrating with complex toolchains and supporting diverse analyst workflows. SOC environments typically feature heterogeneous tool ecosystems that include SIEM platforms, threat intelligence feeds, vulnerability scanners, endpoint detection systems, and network monitoring solutions. Bash scripts serve as integration layers that enable these tools to share data and coordinate activities effectively.

SOC analysts rely heavily on Bash scripting to customize their work environments, automate repetitive analysis tasks, and develop specialized tools that address specific organizational needs. These scripts often evolve organically as analysts identify inefficiencies in standard procedures and develop custom solutions to address them. Over time, successful individual scripts become integrated into team workflows and eventually mature into critical operational components that support entire SOC functions.

The scale of data processing in enterprise SOCs presents unique challenges that Bash scripting is particularly well-suited to address. SOCs typically process millions of security events daily, requiring efficient parsing, filtering, and correlation capabilities that can adapt to changing data formats and evolving threat patterns. Bash scripts provide the flexibility needed to rapidly modify data processing logic while maintaining the performance characteristics required for high-volume operations.

```
#!/bin/bash
# SOC Event Correlation Script
# Processes SIEM alerts and correlates with threat intelligence
SIEM_LOG_DIR="/var/log/siem"
THREAT_INTEL_DB="/opt/threat-intel/indicators.db"
CORRELATION_OUTPUT="/var/log/soc/correlations"
ALERT_THRESHOLD=5
# Function to process SIEM alerts
process_siem_alerts() {
local log_file="$1"
local processed_count=0
while IFS= read -r alert_line; do
# Parse alert components
local timestamp=$(echo "$alert_line" | jq -r '.timestamp')
local source_ip=$(echo "$alert_line" | jq -r '.source_ip')
local alert_type=$(echo "$alert_line" | jq -r '.alert_type')
local severity=$(echo "$alert_line" | jq -r '.severity')
# Check against threat intelligence
if check_threat_intelligence "$source_ip"; then
escalate_alert "$alert_line" "threat_intel_match"
fi
# Check for alert clustering
```

```
local recent_alerts=$(count_recent_alerts "$source_ip" "3600")
if [ "$recent_alerts" -gt "$ALERT_THRESHOLD" ]; then
escalate_alert "$alert_line" "alert_clustering"
fi
((processed_count++))
# Progress reporting for long-running operations
if [ $((processed_count % 1000)) -eq 0 ]; then
echo "Processed $processed_count alerts..."
fi
done < <(tail -f "$log_file" | jq -c '.')
}
# Threat intelligence correlation
check_threat_intelligence() {
local ip_address="$1"
# Query local threat intelligence database
local threat_match=$(sqlite3 "$THREAT_INTEL_DB" \
"SELECT indicator_type, confidence, last_seen FROM indicators
WHERE indicator_value='$ip_address' AND confidence > 7")
if [ -n "$threat_match" ]; then
echo "Threat intelligence match found for $ip_address"
return 0
fi
return 1
}
# Alert escalation function
escalate_alert() {
local alert_data="$1"
local escalation_reason="$2"
local escalation_timestamp=$(date -u +%Y-%m-%dT%H:%M:%SZ)
# Create escalated alert record
local escalated_alert=$(echo "$alert_data" | jq \
—arg reason "$escalation_reason" \
—arg timestamp "$escalation_timestamp" \
'. + {escalation_reason: $reason, escalation_timestamp: $timestamp}')
# Send to high-priority queue
echo "$escalated_alert" >> "$CORRELATION_OUTPUT/escalated_$(date
+%Y%m%d).json"
# Trigger notification system
notify_analysts "$escalated_alert"
```

```
}
```

Cloud Security Operations and Infrastructure Automation

Cloud environments present unique security challenges that Bash scripting is exceptionally well-positioned to address through infrastructure automation, configuration management, and security monitoring. Cloud security teams leverage Bash scripts to interact with cloud provider APIs, automate security configuration across multiple accounts and regions, and implement consistent security policies at scale. These scripts often integrate with cloud-native tools while providing the flexibility needed to adapt to rapidly evolving cloud services and security requirements.

Infrastructure as Code principles align naturally with Bash scripting capabilities, enabling security teams to define and enforce security configurations through version-controlled scripts. These scripts can automatically configure security groups, implement network segmentation, deploy monitoring solutions, and enforce compliance policies across dynamic cloud environments. The ability to rapidly modify and deploy these scripts enables security teams to respond quickly to new threats and changing business requirements.

Cloud security monitoring represents another area where Bash scripting provides significant value through automated data collection, analysis, and response capabilities. Cloud environments generate massive volumes of audit logs, configuration change events, and security alerts that require efficient processing and correlation. Bash scripts provide the performance and flexibility needed to parse diverse log formats, implement custom correlation logic, and trigger appropriate response actions based on detected conditions.

DevSecOps Pipeline Integration

DevSecOps practices increasingly rely on Bash scripting to integrate security controls throughout software development and deployment pipelines. Security teams use scripts to automate security testing, enforce policy compliance, and provide rapid feedback to development teams about potential security issues. These scripts must operate efficiently within CI/CD pipelines while providing comprehensive security coverage that doesn't impede development velocity.

Security gate automation represents a critical application of Bash scripting in DevSecOps environments, where scripts automatically evaluate code commits, container images, and deployment configurations against security policies. These scripts typically integrate multiple security tools including static code analyzers, vulnerability scanners, and configuration assessment tools, providing unified reporting and enforcement mechanisms. The scripts must balance security rigor with development efficiency, implementing intelligent filtering and risk-based decision making that focuses attention on the most critical security issues.

Container security automation relies heavily on Bash scripting to implement security controls across container lifecycle management. Scripts automate image scanning, runtime monitoring, configuration validation, and incident response procedures specific to containerized environments. These scripts must understand container technologies deeply while integrating with orchestration platforms and security tools to provide comprehensive container security coverage.

Lessons from Red Teams and Blue Teams

The adversarial nature of cybersecurity creates unique perspectives on Bash scripting applications, with red teams and blue teams developing complementary yet distinct approaches to leveraging shell scripting capabilities. Red teams focus on offensive capabilities that enable penetration testing, vulnerability exploitation, and security control evasion, while blue teams emphasize defensive capabilities including threat detection, incident response, and security monitoring. Understanding both perspectives provides a comprehensive view of how Bash scripting contributes to overall security effectiveness.

Red team and blue team experiences reveal important lessons about script design, operational security, and effectiveness measurement that apply broadly to security automation. These lessons emerge from real-world testing scenarios where scripts must perform reliably under stress while maintaining stealth, accuracy, and operational effectiveness. The iterative refinement process that both teams undergo provides valuable insights into script optimization, error handling, and adaptability requirements.

Red Team Offensive Automation Strategies

Red teams leverage Bash scripting to automate penetration testing workflows, develop custom exploitation tools, and implement sophisticated attack simulation scenarios. These scripts must operate effectively across diverse target environments while maintaining stealth and avoiding detection by security controls. Red team scripting emphasizes portability, minimal dependencies, and the ability to operate in constrained environments where standard tools might not be available.

Reconnaissance automation represents a foundational application of red team Bash scripting, where scripts systematically gather information about target environments while minimizing detection risk. These scripts typically implement multi-stage reconnaissance workflows that begin with passive information gathering and progressively escalate to more active techniques based on discovered information and acceptable risk levels. The scripts must balance comprehensiveness with operational security, ensuring that reconnaissance activities don't alert defenders prematurely.

Exploitation framework development demonstrates the sophisticated automation capabilities that red teams develop through Bash scripting. These frameworks often integrate multiple exploitation techniques, payload delivery mechanisms, and post-exploitation tools into cohesive attack platforms that can adapt to different target environments. The frameworks emphasize modularity and extensibility, enabling red team members to rapidly develop and deploy custom capabilities for specific engagement requirements.

```
#!/bin/bash
# Red Team Reconnaissance Automation Framework
TARGET_DOMAIN="$1"
OUTPUT_DIR="/tmp/recon_$(date +%s)"
STEALTH_MODE="${STEALTH_MODE:-true}"
MAX_THREADS="${MAX_THREADS:-10}"
# Stealth configuration
if [ "$STEALTH_MODE" = "true" ]; then
NMAP_TIMING="-T2"
REQUEST_DELAY="2"
USER_AGENT="Mozilla/5.0 (Windows NT 10.0; Win64; x64)
AppleWebKit/537.36"
else
NMAP_TIMING="-T4"
REQUEST_DELAY="0.1"
USER_AGENT="ReconBot/1.0"
fi
# Initialize reconnaissance
initialize_recon() {
mkdir -p "$OUTPUT_DIR"/{passive,active,exploitation}
echo "[$(date)] Starting reconnaissance for $TARGET_DOMAIN"
echo "Output directory: $OUTPUT_DIR"
echo "Stealth mode: $STEALTH_MODE"
}
# Passive reconnaissance phase
passive_recon() {
echo "[$(date)] Starting passive reconnaissance..."
# DNS enumeration
```

```
dig +short "$TARGET_DOMAIN" > "$OUTPUT_DIR/passive/
dns_a_records.txt"
dig +short mx "$TARGET_DOMAIN" > "$OUTPUT_DIR/passive/
dns_mx_records.txt"
dig +short txt "$TARGET_DOMAIN" > "$OUTPUT_DIR/passive/
dns_txt_records.txt"
# Subdomain enumeration via certificate transparency
curl -s "https://crt.sh/?q=%25.$TARGET_DOMAIN&output=json" | \
jq -r '.[].name_value' | \
sed 's/\*\.//g' | \
sort -u > "$OUTPUT_DIR/passive/subdomains_ct.txt"
# WHOIS information
whois "$TARGET_DOMAIN" > "$OUTPUT_DIR/passive/whois.txt"
# Social media and public information gathering
search_public_info "$TARGET_DOMAIN"
}
# Active reconnaissance with stealth considerations
active_recon() {
echo "[$(date)] Starting active reconnaissance..."
# Port scanning with timing controls
nmap $NMAP_TIMING -sS—top-ports 1000 \
-oA "$OUTPUT_DIR/active/port_scan" "$TARGET_DOMAIN"
# Service enumeration
nmap $NMAP_TIMING -sV -sC \
—script=default,vuln \
-oA "$OUTPUT_DIR/active/service_scan" "$TARGET_DOMAIN"
# Web application discovery
if check_web_service "$TARGET_DOMAIN"; then
web_recon "$TARGET_DOMAIN"
fi
}
# Web application reconnaissance
web_recon() {
local target="$1"
# Directory brute forcing with rate limiting
gobuster dir -u "http://$target" \
-w /usr/share/wordlists/dirb/common.txt \
-o "$OUTPUT_DIR/active/directories.txt" \
—delay "${REQUEST_DELAY}s" \
```

```
—user-agent "$USER_AGENT"
# Technology identification
whatweb -a 3 "$target" > "$OUTPUT_DIR/active/technology_stack.txt"
# SSL/TLS analysis
if check_https_service "$target"; then
sslscan "$target" > "$OUTPUT_DIR/active/ssl_analysis.txt"
fi
}
```

Post-exploitation automation demonstrates the advanced scripting capabilities that red teams develop for maintaining access, escalating privileges, and exfiltrating data during penetration testing engagements. These scripts must operate effectively in compromised environments while avoiding detection and maintaining operational security. The automation typically includes persistence mechanisms, privilege escalation techniques, and data collection procedures that maximize the value of successful initial access.

Red team automation also emphasizes the importance of operational security in script design, including techniques for avoiding detection, minimizing forensic artifacts, and maintaining communication with command-and-control infrastructure. These considerations influence every aspect of script development, from code obfuscation techniques to communication protocols and data handling procedures.

Blue Team Defensive Automation Techniques

Blue teams develop Bash scripting capabilities focused on threat detection, incident response, and security monitoring that enable rapid response to security incidents while maintaining comprehensive coverage of potential attack vectors. Blue team scripts emphasize reliability, accuracy, and integration with existing security infrastructure while providing the flexibility needed to adapt to evolving threat landscapes.

Threat hunting automation represents a sophisticated application of blue team Bash scripting, where scripts systematically search for indicators of compromise across enterprise environments. These scripts typically implement hypothesis-driven hunting methodologies that combine behavioral analysis, indicator matching, and anomaly detection to identify potential threats that may have evaded traditional security controls. The scripts must process large volumes of data efficiently while maintaining low false positive rates that enable analysts to focus on genuine threats.

Incident response automation enables blue teams to respond rapidly and consistently to security incidents through predefined playbooks and automated response procedures. These scripts typically integrate with SIEM platforms, threat intelligence feeds, and remediation tools to provide coordinated incident response capabilities. The automation must balance speed with accuracy, ensuring that automated responses don't cause additional disruption while providing the rapid containment needed to minimize incident impact.

```
#!/bin/bash
# Blue Team Threat Hunting Automation
HUNT_ID="$(date +%Y%m%d_%H%M%S)_$(uuidgen | cut -d- -f1)"
LOG_SOURCES=("/var/log/auth.log" "/var/log/syslog" "/var/log/apache2/access.log")
IOC_FEED="/opt/threat-intel/current_iocs.txt"
HUNT_RESULTS="/var/log/hunting/$HUNT_ID"
# Initialize hunting session
initialize_hunt() {
mkdir -p "$HUNT_RESULTS"/{findings,raw_data,analysis}
echo "Threat Hunt Session: $HUNT_ID" > "$HUNT_RESULTS/hunt_summary.txt"
echo "Started: $(date)" >> "$HUNT_RESULTS/hunt_summary.txt"
echo "Analyst: $(whoami)" >> "$HUNT_RESULTS/hunt_summary.txt"
}
# Hypothesis: Lateral movement via SSH
hunt_lateral_movement() {
```

```
echo "[$(date)] Hunting for lateral movement indicators..."
# Look for SSH connections between internal hosts
grep "Accepted password\|Accepted publickey" /var/log/auth.log | \
awk '{print $1, $2, $3, $9, $11}' | \
while read month day time user source_ip; do
if is_internal_ip "$source_ip"; then
echo "$month $day $time: User $user from internal IP $source_ip" \
>> "$HUNT_RESULTS/findings/lateral_movement.txt"
fi
done
# Analyze connection patterns
analyze_connection_patterns
}
# Hypothesis: Data exfiltration via unusual network traffic
hunt_data_exfiltration() {
echo "[$(date)] Hunting for data exfiltration indicators..."
# Large outbound transfers during off-hours
netstat -n | grep :443 | grep ESTABLISHED | \
while read proto recv send local_addr foreign_addr state; do
local foreign_ip=$(echo "$foreign_addr" | cut -d: -f1)
if ! is_whitelisted_ip "$foreign_ip"; then
check_transfer_volume "$foreign_ip"
fi
done
}
# IOC matching across multiple log sources
hunt_known_iocs() {
echo "[$(date)] Hunting for known IOCs..."
while IFS= read -r ioc; do
local ioc_type=$(echo "$ioc" | cut -d',' -f1)
local ioc_value=$(echo "$ioc" | cut -d',' -f2)
local confidence=$(echo "$ioc" | cut -d',' -f3)
if [ "$confidence" -gt 7 ]; then
search_ioc_in_logs "$ioc_type" "$ioc_value"
fi
done < "$IOC_FEED"
}
# Advanced log analysis with correlation
correlate_events() {
```

```
echo "[$(date)] Correlating suspicious events..."
# Time-based correlation window (5 minutes)
local correlation_window=300
# Find events within correlation window
find "$HUNT_RESULTS/findings" -name "*.txt" -exec cat {} \; | \
sort -k1,3 | \
while read event_line; do
local event_time=$(extract_timestamp "$event_line")
correlate_with_timeframe "$event_time" "$correlation_window"
done
}
```

Security monitoring automation enables blue teams to maintain continuous vigilance across enterprise environments through automated data collection, analysis, and alerting capabilities. These scripts typically integrate with multiple data sources including network monitoring tools, endpoint detection systems, and cloud service logs to provide comprehensive security coverage. The monitoring automation must balance completeness with performance, ensuring that critical threats are detected quickly without overwhelming analysts with false positives.

Blue team automation also emphasizes the importance of integration with existing security infrastructure, including SIEM platforms, ticketing systems, and communication tools. This integration enables automated responses to coordinate with human analysts and management systems effectively, ensuring that security incidents receive appropriate attention and resources.

Cross-Team Collaboration and Knowledge Sharing

The most effective cybersecurity organizations foster collaboration between red and blue teams that enables knowledge sharing, capability development, and mutual improvement of security practices. Bash scripting often serves as a common language that enables both teams to share techniques, tools, and methodologies while maintaining their distinct operational focuses. This collaboration leads to more robust security programs that benefit from both offensive and defensive perspectives.

Purple team exercises represent formalized collaboration between red and blue teams that often rely heavily on Bash scripting to create realistic attack simulations and validate defensive capabilities. These exercises require scripts that can simulate sophisticated attack techniques while providing detailed logging and analysis capabilities that enable blue teams to evaluate and improve their detection capabilities. The scripting must balance realism with safety, ensuring that exercises don't cause operational disruption while providing meaningful validation of security controls.

Knowledge sharing platforms often emerge around Bash scripting repositories that contain tools, techniques, and methodologies developed by both red and blue teams. These repositories serve as organizational knowledge bases that preserve institutional knowledge while enabling continuous improvement of security capabilities. The platforms typically include documentation, testing procedures, and usage guidelines that enable team members to leverage and extend existing capabilities effectively.

Automating Mundane Tasks at Scale

One of the most valuable applications of Bash scripting in cybersecurity operations involves automating routine tasks that would otherwise consume significant analyst time while providing limited intellectual challenge or skill development. These mundane tasks, while necessary for maintaining security posture, often become bottlenecks that prevent security teams from focusing on higher-value activities such as threat hunting, security architecture, and strategic planning. Effective automation of routine tasks amplifies team capabilities while improving job satisfaction and operational effectiveness.

Scale considerations become particularly important when automating routine tasks across enterprise environments where automation must handle thousands of systems, process millions of events, and coordinate with numerous stakeholders. The automation must be robust enough to handle unexpected conditions while maintaining performance characteristics that meet operational requirements. Additionally, the automation must provide appropriate monitoring and alerting capabilities that ensure continued effectiveness as environments evolve.

Log Processing and Analysis at Enterprise Scale

Log processing represents one of the most common automation targets in cybersecurity operations, where organizations must analyze massive volumes of log data from diverse sources to identify security threats and maintain compliance requirements. Enterprise environments typically generate terabytes of log data daily from network devices, servers, applications, and security tools, creating processing challenges that require sophisticated automation to address effectively.

Distributed log processing architectures leverage Bash scripting to coordinate processing across multiple systems while maintaining data integrity and processing efficiency. These architectures typically implement parallel processing strategies that distribute log parsing tasks across available resources while providing centralized coordination and result aggregation. The scripts must handle various failure scenarios gracefully while maintaining processing throughput that meets operational requirements.

Real-time log analysis automation enables organizations to detect and respond to security threats as they occur rather than waiting for batch processing cycles. These scripts typically implement streaming analysis techniques that process log entries as they are generated while maintaining the performance characteristics needed for high-volume environments. The automation must balance analysis depth with processing speed, ensuring that critical threats are detected quickly without creating processing backlogs.

```
#!/bin/bash
# Enterprise Log Processing Automation Framework
LOG_PROCESSING_DIR="/var/log/processing"
PROCESSED_LOGS_DIR="/var/log/processed"
ALERT_THRESHOLD_DIR="/etc/log-processing/thresholds"
WORKER_COUNT="${WORKER_COUNT:-$(nproc)}"
BATCH_SIZE="${BATCH_SIZE:-1000}"
# Master processing coordinator
coordinate_log_processing() {
echo "Starting distributed log processing with $WORKER_COUNT workers"
# Initialize processing queues
initialize_processing_queues
# Start worker processes
for ((i=1; i<=WORKER_COUNT; i++)); do
start_worker_process "$i" &
WORKER_PIDS+=($!)
done
# Monitor processing status
monitor_processing_status
# Wait for workers to complete
wait "${WORKER_PIDS[@]}"
# Generate processing summary
generate_processing_summary
}
# Individual worker process
start_worker_process() {
local worker_id="$1"
local worker_log="$LOG_PROCESSING_DIR/worker_${worker_id}.log"
echo "Worker $worker_id starting..." > "$worker_log"
while true; do
# Get next batch from queue
local batch_file=$(get_next_batch "$worker_id")
if [ -z "$batch_file" ]; then
sleep 5
continue
fi
# Process batch
process_log_batch "$batch_file" "$worker_id"
# Mark batch as complete
```

```
mark_batch_complete "$batch_file" "$worker_id"
done
}
# Batch processing logic
process_log_batch() {
local batch_file="$1"
local worker_id="$2"
local start_time=$(date +%s)
# Parse different log formats
case "$(detect_log_format "$batch_file")" in
"apache")
process_apache_logs "$batch_file"
;;
"syslog")
process_syslog_entries "$batch_file"
;;
"firewall")
process_firewall_logs "$batch_file"
;;
"auth")
process_authentication_logs "$batch_file"
;;
*)
process_generic_logs "$batch_file"
;;
esac
local end_time=$(date +%s)
local processing_time=$((end_time - start_time))
echo "Worker $worker_id processed $batch_file in ${processing_time}s"
}
# Apache log processing
process_apache_logs() {
local log_file="$1"
local output_file="$PROCESSED_LOGS_DIR/apache_$(basename "$log_file")"
# Extract and analyze web attacks
grep -E "(SELECT|UNION|script|javascript|eval)" "$log_file" | \
while IFS= read -r attack_line; do
analyze_web_attack "$attack_line"
```

```
done > "$output_file.attacks"
# Analyze access patterns
awk '{print $1}' "$log_file" | sort | uniq -c | sort -nr | \
while read count ip; do
if [ "$count" -gt 100 ]; then
echo "High volume access from $ip: $count requests"
fi
done > "$output_file.volume"
# Check for suspicious user agents
awk -F'"' '{print $6}' "$log_file" | sort | uniq -c | \
while read count user_agent; do
if is_suspicious_user_agent "$user_agent"; then
echo "Suspicious user agent: $user_agent (count: $count)"
fi
done > "$output_file.suspicious_agents"
}
```

Automated log correlation enables organizations to identify sophisticated attack patterns that span multiple systems and time periods. These scripts implement complex correlation logic that connects related events across different log sources while maintaining the performance needed for large-scale environments. The correlation automation must handle temporal relationships, pattern matching, and statistical analysis while providing clear explanations of identified relationships.

Log retention and archival automation ensures that organizations maintain appropriate log history while managing storage costs and compliance requirements. These scripts implement intelligent archival strategies that balance accessibility with storage efficiency while maintaining the ability to retrieve historical data for investigation purposes. The automation must coordinate with backup systems and compliance frameworks while providing appropriate access controls and audit trails.

Vulnerability Management Automation

Vulnerability management represents another area where Bash scripting provides significant value through automation of scanning, analysis, prioritization, and remediation workflows. Enterprise vulnerability management programs must coordinate scanning across thousands of systems while analyzing results from multiple vulnerability scanners and correlating findings with asset criticality and threat intelligence. This coordination requires sophisticated automation that can handle the complexity and scale of modern enterprise environments.

Automated vulnerability scanning orchestration enables organizations to maintain comprehensive vulnerability coverage while optimizing scan scheduling and resource utilization. These scripts typically coordinate multiple scanning tools while managing scan conflicts, prioritizing critical assets, and ensuring that scanning activities don't impact business operations. The orchestration must handle various scanner types and configurations while providing unified reporting and analysis capabilities.

Vulnerability prioritization automation helps organizations focus remediation efforts on the most critical vulnerabilities by combining technical severity ratings with business context and threat intelligence. These scripts implement risk-based prioritization algorithms that consider factors such as asset criticality, exploit availability, network exposure, and compensating controls. The prioritization automation must provide clear explanations of prioritization decisions while enabling manual override when business judgment requires different priorities.

```
#!/bin/bash
# Enterprise Vulnerability Management Automation
VULN_SCANNERS=("nessus" "openvas" "qualys")
ASSET_DATABASE="/opt/asset-mgmt/assets.db"
THREAT_INTEL_FEED="/opt/threat-intel/exploits.json"
VULN_REPORTS_DIR="/var/reports/vulnerability"
```

```
# Orchestrate vulnerability scanning across multiple tools
orchestrate_vulnerability_scanning() {
local scan_policy="$1"
local target_group="$2"
echo "Starting vulnerability scan orchestration"
echo "Policy: $scan_policy, Targets: $target_group"
# Get target list from asset database
local targets=$(get_targets_from_group "$target_group")
# Distribute targets across scanners
distribute_scanning_load "$targets"
# Monitor scan progress
monitor_scan_progress
# Consolidate results
consolidate_scan_results
}
# Intelligent scan scheduling
schedule_vulnerability_scans() {
# Get asset criticality ratings
sqlite3 "$ASSET_DATABASE" \
"SELECT hostname, criticality, last_scan FROM assets WHERE active=1" | \
while IFS='|' read hostname criticality last_scan; do
local days_since_scan=$(calculate_days_since "$last_scan")
local required_frequency=$(get_scan_frequency "$criticality")
if [ "$days_since_scan" -gt "$required_frequency" ]; then
schedule_asset_scan "$hostname" "$criticality"
fi
done
}
# Risk-based vulnerability prioritization
prioritize_vulnerabilities() {
local scan_results="$1"
local prioritized_output="$2"
# Load threat intelligence data
local exploit_db=$(load_exploit_intelligence)
# Process each vulnerability finding
jq -c '.vulnerabilities[]' "$scan_results" | \
while IFS= read -r vuln; do
local cve_id=$(echo "$vuln" | jq -r '.cve_id')
local cvss_score=$(echo "$vuln" | jq -r '.cvss_score')
```

```
local affected_host=$(echo "$vuln" | jq -r '.host')
# Calculate risk score
local risk_score=$(calculate_risk_score \
"$cve_id" "$cvss_score" "$affected_host" "$exploit_db")
# Add risk score to vulnerability record
echo "$vuln" | jq—arg score "$risk_score" \
'. + {risk_score: ($score | tonumber)}' \
>> "$prioritized_output"
done
# Sort by risk score and generate priority report
jq -s 'sort_by(-.risk_score)' "$prioritized_output" > \
"$VULN_REPORTS_DIR/prioritized_$(date +%Y%m%d).json"
}
# Automated remediation coordination
coordinate_remediation() {
local priority_vulns="$1"
# Group vulnerabilities by remediation type
jq -r '.[] | select(.risk_score > 8) |
"\(.remediation_type)|\(.host)|\(.cve_id)"' "$priority_vulns" | \
while IFS='|' read remediation_type host cve_id; do
case "$remediation_type" in
"patch")
schedule_patching "$host" "$cve_id"
;;
"configuration")
generate_config_change "$host" "$cve_id"
;;
"mitigation")
implement_compensating_control "$host" "$cve_id"
;;
esac
done
}
```

Remediation tracking automation ensures that identified vulnerabilities are addressed appropriately while maintaining visibility into remediation progress and effectiveness. These scripts coordinate with patch management systems, configuration management tools, and change control processes to ensure that remediation activities are completed and verified. The tracking automation must provide appropriate reporting and escalation capabilities that ensure accountability and timely resolution of critical vulnerabilities.

Compliance Automation and Reporting

Compliance automation represents a critical application area where Bash scripting enables organizations to maintain regulatory compliance while minimizing the manual effort required for evidence collection and reporting. Compliance frameworks such as PCI DSS, SOX, HIPAA, and SOC 2 require extensive documentation and regular assessment of security controls, creating automation opportunities that significantly reduce compliance overhead while improving accuracy and consistency.

Automated compliance assessment scripts systematically evaluate system configurations, access controls, and security policies against regulatory requirements while generating detailed evidence packages that support audit activities. These scripts must understand specific compliance requirements deeply while providing clear documentation of assessment procedures and results. The automation must handle various system types and configurations while maintaining the accuracy and completeness required for regulatory compliance.

Continuous compliance monitoring enables organizations to maintain compliance posture between formal audit cycles through automated monitoring of control effectiveness and configuration drift. These scripts implement ongoing assessment procedures that detect compliance violations quickly while providing remediation guidance and escalation procedures. The monitoring must balance comprehensiveness with operational efficiency while providing clear reporting that enables proactive compliance management.

Interview Prep: Scripting Questions in Cybersecurity Roles

Technical interviews for cybersecurity positions increasingly emphasize practical scripting abilities that demonstrate both technical competence and problem-solving capabilities relevant to real-world security challenges. Interviewers seek candidates who can translate security requirements into effective automation solutions while demonstrating understanding of both technical implementation details and broader security implications. Preparation for these interviews requires developing fluency in common scripting patterns while understanding how they apply to specific cybersecurity contexts.

Modern cybersecurity interviews often include hands-on scripting exercises that simulate real-world scenarios, requiring candidates to develop solutions under time pressure while explaining their approach and decision-making process. These exercises reveal not only technical abilities but also problem-solving methodologies, code organization skills, and understanding of security best practices. Successful candidates demonstrate the ability to quickly analyze requirements, design appropriate solutions, and implement them efficiently while considering security implications.

The evolution of cybersecurity roles has created demand for professionals who can bridge technical implementation with strategic security thinking, making scripting competency a differentiating factor in competitive job markets. Organizations value candidates who can automate routine tasks, develop custom security tools, and integrate disparate systems through scripting while maintaining appropriate security posture and operational efficiency.

Common Technical Interview Questions and Solutions

Cybersecurity technical interviews typically include a progression of scripting questions that start with fundamental concepts and advance to complex real-world scenarios. Initial questions often focus on basic

Bash syntax, file manipulation, and text processing capabilities before advancing to security-specific applications such as log analysis, network monitoring, and incident response automation. Understanding this progression helps candidates prepare appropriate examples and explanations.

Log analysis questions represent one of the most common interview topics, as log processing skills directly translate to everyday security operations. Interviewers often present sample log files and ask candidates to extract specific information, identify patterns, or detect anomalies through scripting. These questions test both technical implementation skills and security analysis capabilities while revealing candidates' understanding of common attack patterns and detection methodologies.

Network security automation questions typically involve parsing network data, analyzing traffic patterns, or automating security tool interactions. These questions assess candidates' understanding of network protocols, security tools, and automation techniques while evaluating their ability to develop practical solutions for common security challenges. Successful responses demonstrate both technical competency and security domain knowledge.

```
#!/bin/bash
# Interview Question: Analyze web server logs for security incidents
# Sample question: "Write a script that analyzes Apache access logs
# to identify potential security threats and generate a summary report"
LOG_FILE="$1"
REPORT_FILE="${2:-security_report.txt}"
SUSPICIOUS_THRESHOLD=50
analyze_security_threats() {
echo "Security Analysis Report" > "$REPORT_FILE"
echo "Generated: $(date)" >> "$REPORT_FILE"
echo "Log file: $LOG_FILE" >> "$REPORT_FILE"
echo "========================================" >>
"$REPORT_FILE"
# 1. Identify SQL injection attempts
echo -e "\n1. SQL Injection Attempts:" >> "$REPORT_FILE"
```

```
grep -iE "(union|select|insert|delete|drop|script|javascript)" "$LOG_FILE" | \
awk '{print $1, $4, $7}' | \
sort | uniq -c | sort -nr | \
head -10 >> "$REPORT_FILE"
# 2. Detect brute force attacks
echo -e "\n2. Potential Brute Force Sources:" >> "$REPORT_FILE"
awk '{print $1}' "$LOG_FILE" | \
sort | uniq -c | \
awk -v threshold="$SUSPICIOUS_THRESHOLD" \
'$1 > threshold {print $1, $2}' | \
sort -nr >> "$REPORT_FILE"
# 3. Identify suspicious user agents
echo -e "\n3. Suspicious User Agents:" >> "$REPORT_FILE"
awk -F'"' '{print $6}' "$LOG_FILE" | \
sort | uniq -c | \
grep -iE "(bot|crawler|scanner|nikto|sqlmap)" | \
sort -nr >> "$REPORT_FILE"
# 4. Analyze HTTP response codes
echo -e "\n4. HTTP Response Code Analysis:" >> "$REPORT_FILE"
awk '{print $9}' "$LOG_FILE" | \
sort | uniq -c | \
sort -nr >> "$REPORT_FILE"
# 5. Find directory traversal attempts
echo -e "\n5. Directory Traversal Attempts:" >> "$REPORT_FILE"
grep -E "(\.\./|\.\.\\\\)" "$LOG_FILE" | \
awk '{print $1, $7}' | \
sort | uniq >> "$REPORT_FILE"
}
# Interview follow-up: Explain how you would enhance this script
enhancement_suggestions() {
cat << EOF
Enhancement Suggestions:
1. Add GeoIP lookup for source IP analysis
2. Implement time-based correlation analysis
3. Add integration with threat intelligence feeds
4. Include automated alerting for critical threats
5. Add configuration file for customizable thresholds
6. Implement real-time monitoring capabilities
7. Add database storage for historical analysis
```

```
EOF
}
# Demonstrate error handling and input validation
validate_input() {
if [ $# -eq 0 ]; then
echo "Usage: $0 <log_file> [report_file]"
echo "Example: $0 /var/log/apache2/access.log security_report.txt"
exit 1
fi
if [ ! -f "$LOG_FILE" ]; then
echo "Error: Log file '$LOG_FILE' not found"
exit 1
fi
if [ ! -r "$LOG_FILE" ]; then
echo "Error: Cannot read log file '$LOG_FILE'"
exit 1
fi
}
# Main execution
main() {
validate_input "$@"
analyze_security_threats
echo "Security analysis complete. Report saved to: $REPORT_FILE"
}
# Only execute if script is run directly (not sourced)
if [ "${BASH_SOURCE[0]}" = "${0}" ]; then
main "$@"
fi
```

Incident response automation questions challenge candidates to develop scripts that can rapidly collect forensic evidence, contain threats, or coordinate response activities. These questions assess understanding of incident response procedures, forensic principles, and automation best practices while evaluating candidates' ability to work under pressure. Strong responses demonstrate both technical implementation skills and strategic thinking about incident response workflows.

System hardening and compliance automation represents another common interview theme, where candidates must demonstrate ability to assess system configurations, implement security controls, and maintain compliance through scripting. These questions test understanding of security baselines, configuration management, and regulatory requirements while assessing automation design and implementation capabilities.

Behavioral Questions and Problem-Solving Scenarios

Behavioral interview questions in cybersecurity contexts often explore how candidates have used scripting to solve real-world security challenges, overcome technical obstacles, or improve operational efficiency. These questions seek to understand candidates' problem-solving approaches, learning agility, and ability to work effectively in team environments while leveraging automation capabilities.

Scenario-based questions present complex security challenges that require candidates to design comprehensive automation solutions while considering multiple constraints and requirements. These scenarios typically involve multiple stakeholders, competing priorities, and technical limitations that require creative problem-solving and clear communication. Successful responses demonstrate ability to analyze complex requirements, design appropriate solutions, and explain technical decisions to non-technical stakeholders.

Collaboration and knowledge sharing questions explore how candidates work with team members, share automation solutions, and contribute to organizational knowledge bases. These questions assess communication skills, teamwork capabilities, and commitment to continuous learning while understanding how candidates approach documentation, training, and mentoring responsibilities.

Technical Assessment and Coding Challenges

Live coding exercises represent increasingly common interview components where candidates must develop scripting solutions in real-time while explaining their thought process and decision-making. These exercises reveal not only coding abilities but also debugging skills, problem-solving approaches, and ability to work under pressure. Preparation for live coding requires practicing common patterns while developing confidence in explaining technical decisions.

Code review exercises present existing scripts with intentional errors, security vulnerabilities, or inefficiencies that candidates must identify and address. These exercises test debugging skills, security knowledge, and understanding of best practices while assessing ability to analyze and improve existing code. Strong performance requires systematic code analysis techniques combined with comprehensive understanding of security implications.

Architecture design questions challenge candidates to design automation frameworks or integration solutions that address complex organizational requirements. These questions assess system design capabilities, understanding of scalability considerations, and ability to balance competing requirements while maintaining security and operational effectiveness. Successful responses demonstrate both technical depth and strategic thinking about long-term automation strategies.

Portfolio Development and Demonstration Projects

Building a portfolio of scripting projects provides concrete evidence of capabilities while demonstrating passion for cybersecurity automation and continuous learning. Effective portfolios include diverse projects that showcase different aspects of security automation while providing clear documentation and explanation of design decisions. The portfolio should demonstrate progression in complexity and sophistication while highlighting specific achievements and learning outcomes.

GitHub repositories serve as excellent platforms for showcasing scripting capabilities while demonstrating familiarity with version control and collaborative development practices. Repository organization, documentation quality, and commit history provide insights into candidates' development practices and attention to detail. Well-maintained repositories demonstrate professionalism and commitment to quality that distinguish strong candidates.

Contribution to open-source security projects provides valuable experience while building reputation within the cybersecurity community. These contributions demonstrate ability to work with existing codebases, follow established conventions, and collaborate with distributed teams. Open-source contributions also provide networking opportunities and learning experiences that enhance overall cybersecurity capabilities.

Industry Certifications and Continuing Education

Professional certifications increasingly include scripting and automation components that validate practical capabilities while demonstrating commitment to professional development. Certifications such as GCIH, GCFA, and GPEN include hands-on components that require scripting skills while providing structured learning paths for developing automation capabilities. Understanding certification requirements helps guide skill development while providing credential recognition.

Continuing education through conferences, workshops, and online training provides ongoing skill development while maintaining awareness of emerging trends and technologies. The rapidly evolving cybersecurity landscape requires continuous learning to maintain relevance and effectiveness. Active engagement with the cybersecurity community through conferences and training demonstrates commitment to professional growth while providing networking opportunities.

Industry recognition through presentations, publications, or community leadership positions provides credibility while demonstrating expertise and communication skills. Sharing knowledge through blog posts, conference presentations, or training sessions establishes thought leadership while contributing to the broader cybersecurity community. These activities provide valuable experience while building professional reputation and network.

Career Progression and Specialization Paths

Understanding career progression paths in cybersecurity helps candidates align skill development with long-term goals while demonstrating awareness of industry trends and opportunities. Different specialization areas such as incident response, threat hunting, or security architecture require different automation capabilities and skill emphases. Clear understanding of specialization requirements enables focused skill development and strategic career planning.

Leadership preparation involves developing not only technical capabilities but also project management, team leadership, and strategic planning skills that enable progression into senior roles. Security leaders must understand both technical implementation details and business implications while being able to communicate effectively with stakeholders at all levels. Automation capabilities provide foundation for leadership roles while enabling teams to scale effectively.

Entrepreneurial opportunities in cybersecurity increasingly involve automation and tool development capabilities that enable independent consulting or product development. Understanding market needs, customer requirements, and business development principles provides foundation for entrepreneurial success while leveraging technical automation capabilities. Many successful cybersecurity entrepreneurs begin with strong automation skills that enable them to solve real-world problems effectively.

Advanced Case Study Analysis

Examining detailed case studies from real-world cybersecurity implementations provides valuable insights into how organizations successfully leverage Bash scripting to address complex security challenges while achieving measurable improvements in operational efficiency and security effectiveness. These case studies reveal not only technical implementation details but also organizational factors, change management considerations, and lessons learned that influence automation success.

The most successful automation implementations typically begin with clear problem definition, stakeholder alignment, and realistic scope definition before progressing to technical design and implementation. Understanding this progression helps security professionals approach automation projects systematically while avoiding common pitfalls that can derail automation initiatives. The case studies also reveal how successful organizations measure and communicate automation value to ensure continued support and resources.

Fortune 500 Enterprise Security Transformation

A major financial services organization faced challenges managing security across a hybrid infrastructure comprising on-premises data centers, multiple cloud providers, and numerous acquired subsidiaries with different security toolsets. The organization needed to achieve consistent security monitoring, automated compliance reporting, and coordinated incident response across this complex environment while maintaining regulatory compliance and operational efficiency.

The transformation initiative began with comprehensive assessment of existing security tools, processes, and skill sets across the organization. This assessment revealed significant gaps in automation capabilities, inconsistent security monitoring coverage, and manual processes that created operational bottlenecks and compliance risks.

The organization decided to implement a comprehensive automation framework built primarily on Bash scripting with strategic integration of Python and cloud-native tools.

The implementation strategy emphasized incremental deployment with clear success metrics and stakeholder communication at each phase. The first phase focused on log aggregation and basic security monitoring automation that provided immediate value while building confidence in the automation approach. Subsequent phases added vulnerability management automation, compliance reporting, and incident response capabilities while gradually expanding coverage across the entire organization.

```
#!/bin/bash
# Enterprise Security Orchestration Framework
# Case Study: Financial Services Multi-Cloud Environment
ENVIRONMENTS=("prod" "staging" "dev" "dr")
CLOUD_PROVIDERS=("aws" "azure" "gcp")
SUBSIDIARIES=("subsidiary-a" "subsidiary-b" "subsidiary-c")
# Multi-environment security orchestration
orchestrate_security_operations() {
local operation="$1"
shift
local targets=("$@")
echo "Starting security operation: $operation"
echo "Targets: ${targets[*]}"
# Initialize operation tracking
local operation_id=$(generate_operation_id)
local results_dir="/var/security/operations/$operation_id"
mkdir -p "$results_dir"
# Execute operation across all environments
for environment in "${ENVIRONMENTS[@]}"; do
for provider in "${CLOUD_PROVIDERS[@]}"; do
for subsidiary in "${SUBSIDIARIES[@]}"; do
execute_environment_operation \
"$operation" "$environment" "$provider" "$subsidiary" \
"$results_dir" &
done
done
```

```
done
# Wait for all operations to complete
wait
# Consolidate and analyze results
consolidate_operation_results "$operation_id" "$results_dir"
}
# Environment-specific operation execution
execute_environment_operation() {
local operation="$1"
local environment="$2"
local provider="$3"
local subsidiary="$4"
local results_dir="$5"
local context="${environment}-${provider}-${subsidiary}"
local log_file="$results_dir/${context}.log"
echo "Executing $operation for $context" > "$log_file"
# Load environment-specific configuration
load_environment_config "$environment" "$provider" "$subsidiary"
case "$operation" in
"vulnerability_scan")
execute_vulnerability_scan "$context" "$log_file"
;;
"compliance_check")
execute_compliance_assessment "$context" "$log_file"
;;
"security_monitoring")
execute_security_monitoring "$context" "$log_file"
;;
"incident_response")
execute_incident_response "$context" "$log_file"
;;
esac
}
# Results consolidation and reporting
consolidate_operation_results() {
local operation_id="$1"
local results_dir="$2"
# Generate executive summary
cat > "$results_dir/executive_summary.txt" << EOF
```

```
Security Operation Summary
Operation ID: $operation_id
Completion Time: $(date)
Environments Processed: ${#ENVIRONMENTS[@]}
Cloud Providers: ${#CLOUD_PROVIDERS[@]}
Subsidiaries: ${#SUBSIDIARIES[@]}
Total Scope: $((${#ENVIRONMENTS[@]} *
${#CLOUD_PROVIDERS[@]} * ${#SUBSIDIARIES[@]})) contexts
EOF
# Aggregate findings across all contexts
find "$results_dir" -name "*.log" -exec grep -l "CRITICAL" {} \; | \
wc -l > "$results_dir/critical_findings_count.txt"
find "$results_dir" -name "*.log" -exec grep -l "HIGH" {} \; | \
wc -l > "$results_dir/high_findings_count.txt"
# Generate compliance dashboard
generate_compliance_dashboard "$results_dir"
# Send notifications to stakeholders
notify_stakeholders "$operation_id" "$results_dir"
}
```

The implementation achieved significant improvements in security posture and operational efficiency. Automated security monitoring reduced mean time to detection from hours to minutes while providing consistent coverage across all environments. Compliance reporting automation reduced quarterly reporting effort from weeks to days while improving accuracy and audit trail completeness. Incident response automation enabled coordinated response across multiple environments while maintaining detailed forensic evidence.

Key success factors included strong executive sponsorship, dedicated automation team with both security and development expertise, comprehensive training program for security analysts, and iterative implementation approach that delivered value incrementally. The organization also invested heavily in documentation, testing, and change management to ensure sustainable automation capabilities.

Startup Security Automation Bootstrap

A rapidly growing technology startup needed to implement comprehensive security capabilities while maintaining lean operational overhead and supporting aggressive growth targets. The organization faced typical startup constraints including limited budget, small team size, and rapidly changing infrastructure while needing to achieve enterprise-grade security capabilities for customer confidence and regulatory compliance.

The startup's approach emphasized open-source tools, cloud-native services, and extensive automation to achieve security capabilities that would typically require much larger teams. Bash scripting served as the primary automation language due to its ubiquity, minimal dependencies, and ability to integrate easily with cloud services and existing tools. The team developed a comprehensive automation framework that provided security monitoring, vulnerability management, and compliance capabilities with minimal ongoing operational overhead.

The implementation strategy prioritized automation from the beginning rather than attempting to automate existing manual processes. This approach enabled the startup to achieve security capabilities that scaled automatically with infrastructure growth while avoiding the technical debt associated with retrofitting automation onto existing manual processes. The automation framework provided foundation for security operations that could support the organization through rapid growth phases.

Government Agency Modernization Initiative

A federal government agency undertook modernization of legacy security infrastructure while maintaining strict compliance requirements and operating within constrained budget allocations. The agency needed to replace aging security tools with modern capabilities while ensuring continuity of operations and maintaining extensive audit trails required for government oversight.

The modernization approach emphasized gradual migration with parallel operation of legacy and modern systems during transition periods. Bash scripting provided integration capabilities that enabled new automation systems to work with legacy tools while gradually replacing manual processes with automated alternatives. The scripting framework also provided detailed logging and audit capabilities required for government compliance frameworks.

Implementation challenges included stringent security requirements, extensive approval processes, and integration with classified systems that required specialized handling. The agency addressed these challenges through comprehensive security review processes, incremental deployment strategies, and extensive testing procedures that validated automation behavior under various scenarios. The resulting automation framework provided significant operational improvements while maintaining compliance with government security requirements.

Conclusion

The real-world case studies and practical applications explored in this chapter demonstrate the transformative impact that Bash scripting can have on cybersecurity operations when applied systematically and strategically. From enterprise-scale security orchestration to startup automation frameworks, the examples reveal common patterns and principles that enable successful automation implementations across diverse organizational contexts. The key to success lies not in the complexity of individual scripts but in the systematic approach to identifying automation opportunities, designing scalable solutions, and implementing them with appropriate consideration for operational requirements and constraints.

The lessons learned from red team and blue team experiences highlight the importance of understanding both offensive and defensive perspectives when developing security automation capabilities. This dual perspective enables security professionals to create more robust and effective automation solutions while anticipating potential limitations and attack vectors. The collaborative approaches emerging between traditionally adversarial teams demonstrate how shared automation capabilities can enhance overall security effectiveness while fostering knowledge sharing and continuous improvement.

The progression from mundane task automation to sophisticated security orchestration illustrates how organizations can build automation capabilities incrementally while achieving measurable improvements in operational efficiency and security effectiveness. The most successful implementations begin with clear problem definition and stakeholder alignment before progressing through systematic design, implementation, and optimization phases. This approach enables organizations to achieve sustainable automation capabilities that provide long-term value while adapting to evolving security challenges.

The interview preparation guidance and technical assessment examples provide practical framework for developing and demonstrating scripting capabilities in professional contexts. The emphasis on both technical implementation skills and strategic thinking reflects the evolving nature of cybersecurity roles where professionals must bridge technical execution with business objectives. Understanding these expectations enables security professionals to develop comprehensive capabilities that support career advancement while contributing to organizational security effectiveness.

As cybersecurity continues to evolve with new threats, technologies, and regulatory requirements, the ability to rapidly develop and deploy custom automation solutions becomes increasingly valuable. The case studies and examples presented in this chapter provide foundation for building sophisticated automation capabilities while understanding the organizational factors that influence automation success. The investment in developing comprehensive scripting skills pays dividends not only in immediate operational improvements but also in enhanced career opportunities and ability to adapt to changing cybersecurity landscapes.

The future of cybersecurity operations will increasingly depend on the ability to combine human expertise with automated capabilities that provide scalable, consistent, and effective security coverage. Bash scripting provides an accessible yet powerful foundation for building these capabilities while maintaining the flexibility needed to adapt to emerging challenges. The professionals who master these capabilities while understanding their strategic application will be well-positioned to lead the next generation of cybersecurity operations and contribute to the ongoing evolution of security practices and methodologies.

Don't miss out!

Visit the website below and you can sign up to receive emails whenever Rick Stupart publishes a new book. There's no charge and no obligation.

https://books2read.com/r/B-A-CSFOD-YYUQJ

BOOKS 2 READ

Connecting independent readers to independent writers.

Also by Rick Stupart

Built to Fail: The Tacoma Narrows Bridge Disaster Why Engineers Shouldn't Design for Wind by Guessing
Four Lives Lost: The Bryan Kohberger Idaho Murders Case
The Money Delusion
Defense In Depth: Building Layered Security For Home, Business, And Beyond
Ghost In The Machine: Stuxnet Revealed
Paper Fortunes: The Frenchman Who Tried To Buy An Empire
Thomas Midgley Jr.: The Man Who Accidentally Destroyed the Atmosphere
Shell Shocked: Learn Bash for Cybersecurity and Automation

Watch for more at https://www.elcpublishing.com.

About the Author

David G. Stone is a seasoned researcher and IT professional with over 20 years of experience in information technology, cybersecurity, and risk management. Holding a master's degree in Information Systems Management, David G. Stone has spent years helping businesses and individuals navigate the complex world of digital security.

As a CompTIA CySA+ certified cybersecurity expert, David G. Stone specializes in threat detection, vulnerability management, and security best practices. With extensive experience implementing the NIST Cybersecurity Framework, they have worked with organizations to strengthen their security posture and protect sensitive data from cyber threats.

Passionate about educating others, David G. Stone has now turned their expertise into an easy-to-follow guide designed to help remote workers, freelancers, and businesses safeguard their online accounts. Through The Remote Worker's Guide to Password Management, they provide practical, real-world strategies to enhance digital security and prevent cyber risks.

When not working in cybersecurity, David G. Stone explores emerging technologies, consults on IT risk management, developing innovative solutions for businesses, and writing. With a deep passion for money, history, economics, and business, David brings a sharp, curious mind to the page—blending engaging narrative with thoughtful analysis. A new writer with ELC Publishing, he is committed to turning his long-held interests and extensive published work into books that inform, entertain, and provoke reflection.

Read more at https://www.elcpublishing.com.

www.ingramcontent.com/pod-product-compliance
Lightning Source LLC
LaVergne TN
LVHW050747061126
851857LV00026B/719